pirates of the Atlantic

Robbery, murder and mayhem off the Canadian East Coast

Dan Conlin

FORMAC PUBLISHING COMPANY LTD.

Formac Publishing Company Limited recognizes the support of the Province of Nova Scotia through the Department of Tourism, Culture and Heritage. We acknowledge the financial support of the Government of Canada through the Book Publishing Industry Development Program (BPIDP) for our publishing activities. Formac Publishing Company Limited acknowledges the support of the Canada Council for the Arts for our publishing program.

Canada Council Conseil des Arts
for the Arts du Canada

NOVA SCOTIA
Tourism, Culture and Heritage

Library and Archives Canada Cataloguing in Publication

Conlin, Dan (Daniel), 1964-
        Pirates of the Atlantic : robbery, murder and mayhem off the Canadian east coast / Dan Conlin.

ISBN 978-0-88780-741-1

        1. Pirates—Atlantic Coast (Canada) —History.   2. Piracy—Atlantic Coast (Canada) —History.   3. Pirates—Biography.   4. Atlantic Coast (Canada) —History. I. Title.

FC2019.P57C66 2008   909'.096344   C2008-903850-9

Formac Publishing Company Limited
5502 Atlantic Street
Halifax, Nova Scotia
B3H 1G4
www.formac.ca

Printed and bound in China

CONTENTS

This symbol indicates a photo or artifact found in the collection of the Maritime Museum of the Atlantic in Halifax, Nova Scotia.

ACKNOWLEDGEMENTS

Like many people in Nova Scotia, I was first inspired by the legends of piracy that I heard in childhood, from my grandmother Christy Schaffner and mother Mary Louise Conlin. Professionally, I am indebted to historians John Read and Colin Howell at Saint Mary's University in Halifax, who first introduced me to the serious scholarship about piracy that exists beyond its colourful legends. They planted the seeds of an exhibit that I curated at the Maritime Museum of the Atlantic in Halifax, Nova Scotia, in 2007 entitled "Pirates: Myth and Reality," which inspired this book. This exhibit was made possible by the wise leadership of Museum Director Marven Moore, the energetic exhibit management of Gerry Lunn and the talented design of Stephen Slipp. It was enhanced by the great pirate knowledge of museum interpreters Andrew Aulenback and Derek Harrison. Museum Research Associate David Walker provided vital commentary. Most significantly I have benefited from the dedicated stewardship of the Maritime Museum of the Atlantic's Registrar Lynn-Marie Richard, who has kept the Museum's rare collection of pirate artifacts accessible and secure. I have similarly benefited from the generous help of Scott Robson, Curator, and Sheila Yeoman, Registrar, of the Nova Scotia Museum's History Collection; Kevin Robbin at the Army Museum; and staff at the Nova Scotia Archives and Records Management, especially Gary Shutlak and Anjali Vohra. Vital help was also provided by Halifax Public Libraries Reference Librarian Joanne McCarthy and Jeanne Howell at the Cambridge Military Library, one of the city's overlooked research treasures. Mac Mackay, who publishes *Shipfax*, the great insider newsletter on Halifax shipping, was a big help on modern piracy. Nova Scotia is also home to one of the great international authorities on piracy, the artist and author of *Pirate's Passage*, William Gilkerson, who generously shared his knowledge and collection of pirate artifacts. Above all, I am grateful for the commentary and inspiration provided by my wife Patricia Acheson, without whom this book would not have been possible.

INTRODUCTION

Bartholomew Roberts' dawn entry into the busy fishing harbour of Trepassey, Newfoundland, on June 21, 1720, was unforgettable. About 22 ships were anchored at the settlement to the south of St. John's. As the day dawned, fishermen were making ready in the 150 boats of the inshore fleet when Roberts arrived in his sloop, *Fortune*, drums beating and trumpets sounding. From one mast flew English colours, but from the other waved Roberts' black flag with its skull and cutlass. The hills echoed to a steady cannonade from *Fortune*'s ten guns. The ships in the harbour mounted more than 40 guns, but their crews all knew of Roberts' reputation and fled ashore as fast as they could row.

After two riotous weeks, Roberts and his now greatly enlarged band of pirates sailed away to plunder Newfoundland and Nova Scotian waters for months. His hundreds of followers, including many Newfoundland fishermen, would scour the Atlantic for two more years until their end in a bloody battle off the coast of Africa.

Roberts was one of many pirates to haunt the waters of Atlantic Canada at the height of piracy's Golden Age. Their deeds became so legendary that to many Canadians today pirates are perhaps more mythical than real. Atlantic Canada is steeped in pirate legend and those who live there share the widespread fascination with the image of pirates in popular culture. However the region has a deep history of real pirates, including some of the best-known and cruellest names in the trade. Roberts' raid at Trepassey was very real to his victims, just as piracy remains a very real threat today in many parts of the world.

Although law courts have sometimes struggled to define piracy, for generations of seafarers on the North Atlantic it was the well-understood and well-feared crime of violent robbery at sea. In fact, at the peak of European piracy in the early 1700s, desperate British lawmakers expanded the definition of piracy to include almost every crime at sea. Theft, mutiny, treason, trading with pirates and even failure to vigorously resist pirates were defined by law as piracy and subject to merciless punishment.

As states became more powerful, the definition of piracy was reduced in scope, and today criminal charges of theft and murder are usually applied to pirates. However piracy remains on the books of most nations as an especially serious category of crime with its own special laws, since the vastness of the ocean makes pirates hard to catch and the damage they can inflict on trade makes their crimes a special threat.

Throughout much of history piracy was one end of a spectrum of violence at sea perpetrated by three broad categories: navies, state-sanctioned private raiders and pirates, although to a ship under attack, the identity of the predator was often academic.

Navies comprise warships owned and

directly controlled by government. They are capable of great carnage but are expensive and usually afforded by only the largest states. A more affordable option, but one that is harder for states to control, is to sanction raiders called at various times corsairs, buccaneers or privateers. Their ships were privately owned but government controlled, to a greater or lesser degree. In exchange for attacking enemy ships, governments let them keep most of what they captured. They cost the state nothing but could sometimes drift into the other category, piracy.

True pirates are stateless criminals who prey on anyone in war or peace. Their ships, owned by the pirates themselves, are controlled by no one. In their own words, pirates "declare war on all the world."

While many naval sailors and privateers carried out bloody and terrible deeds, they were all enlisted in one way or another to serve the state. This book is about the true pirates, outlaws who defiantly served no state, but only themselves. The pirates of myth fascinate us with images of romantic freedom, daring rebellion and treasure. The pirates of reality were cruel, desperate and mostly short-lived criminals. This book seeks to chart their lives and raids in Atlantic Canadian waters and separate them from their thick cloak of romance, while also understanding where that romance comes from.

Chapter One explores how piracy came to Atlantic Canada and follows the privateers who turned pirate. Chapters Two to Four focus on the Golden Age of Piracy through the lives of three formidable pirates who raided the waters of Atlantic Canada. Chapter Five looks at pirates in the Age of Sail, as well as mutineers who took their own ships and wreckers who robbed shipwrecks. Chapter Six explores some of the realities of pirate life, and especially pirate codes of conduct. Chapters Seven and Eight examine myths about piracy that have evolved in folklore and popular culture. Finally, the Postscript takes a brief look at the pirates who are still very much alive and operating on the oceans of the world today.

Innocent merchant ship or pirate in disguise? An approaching tall ship replica evokes the mariner's age-old worry.

BUCCANEERS AND PRIVATEERS

Beyond the line there are no more friends and anything afloat is a prize.

Étienne de Flacourt, Governor of Madagascar, 1658

Piracy is as old as the ocean. It appears with the first written accounts of trade and travel and continues today. Egyptian hieroglyphs detail raids by the "Sea Peoples" who raided Egypt's coasts. Most famously, Julius Caesar was captured twice by Cilician pirates. After they spared his life on payment of a ransom in 75 BC, he promptly tracked them down and crucified them. His great political rival, Pompey, owed much of his political success to the build-up of the Roman Navy, which crushed Mediterranean Piracy in 67 BC.

When Rome fell, piracy flourished again in northern Europe. Bands of Basque, Irish, Saxon and especially Viking pirates raided for centuries. In the Mediterranean, Christian pirates based in Malta captured Moslems for the slave trades, while Arab-harboured raiders known as Barbary Pirates took Christian slaves and loot from European ships. European navies were slow to evolve and at first could only be afforded by a few giant empires, such as that of Spain.

Piracy in Atlantic Canada arrived with the rival European empires that sought to conquer and settle North America. Many of the Europeans who first arrived in Atlantic Canada in the late 1500s and early 1600s sought trade

Even the imperious Julius Caesar was briefly captured by pirates, until he exacted crushing retribution.

lapping patchwork of rival claims by Basque, Portuguese, Spanish, French and English governments resulted in constant rivalry. Often colonial powers attacked rival settlements regardless of whether their home nations in Europe were at peace.

"No peace over the line!" was the declaration of the French, English and Dutch mariners who crossed the Tordesillas Line. This was a north-south line established by a Spanish and Portuguese treaty in 1494, which gave Spain almost all of North and South America. Spain for a time had the world's richest empire. Gold and silver flowed in mind-boggling quantities from her vast conquered colonies on the American mainland, the fabled "Spanish Main." Spanish currency, such as gold doubloons and the silver dollars known as "Pieces of Eight," flooded the Atlantic world through illegal trade and buccaneering raids. Spanish money became the *de facto* world currency of the time.

English raiders such as Francis Drake and John Hawkins in the 1500s were the first to challenge Spain, but the most sustained attacks came in the 1600s. Small bands of English, French and Dutch hunters camped on Caribbean islands where they hunted and smoked meat. They were known as *boucaniers*, the French word for "hunters of smoked meat," soon pronounced as "buccaneers" in English. When Spain brutally attacked their hunting settlements, the buccaneers banded together in large numbers to attack Spanish shipping and towns.

The small English, French and Dutch colonies in the Caribbean were quick to use these raiders

and treaties with the native peoples of the region. But many others were little more than heavily armed bands of pirates. One after another they stole, killed, kidnapped and enforced bold claims with unpredictable violence.

European governments claimed and then settled Atlantic Canada indirectly, using private adventurers and companies armed with far-ranging but ill-controlled powers. An over-to weaken the giant Spanish empire. Buccaneers were given supplies, arms and legal authority to attack the Spanish with special licenses called "Letters of Marque." These licenses contained restrictions on which ships could be captured and were supposed to require that captures, called "prizes," be brought before a court for scrutiny. A buccaneer with a Letter of Marque was a "privateer," a licensed private warship fighting for the state. A buccaneer without a Letter of Marque was a pirate. However these licenses were often traded, falsified and frequently ignored, as the tiny colonies in North America had no courts or navies to enforce them. Buccaneers drifted back and forth from legal privateer to illegal pirate with little consequence as long as they were successful.

Given almost *carte blanche* to attack the Spanish, buccaneers mounted large scale and often murderous raids in the Caribbean. They were led most memorably by Henry Morgan in the late 1600s. Morgan epitomized the buccaneering era with his successful, although not always legal, raids on Spanish colonies. His activities, for a time, landed him with the governorship of Jamaica.

Similar, almost lawless colonial rivalries also existed to the north in Atlantic Canada. By the 1600s, Atlantic Canada was mostly populated by still-powerful native peoples. The few tiny colonies in Nova Scotia and Newfoundland were dwarfed by a massive seasonal fishery. Tens of

Hero to the English, pirate to the Spanish: Francis Drake is immortalized by this statue in Plymouth, England, and a 19th century engraving of his ships attacking a Spanish treasure fleet.

Above: The entrance to St. John's Harbour, a frequent pirate target, with Fort Amherst, its defense in later years. Opposite: Illustrator Howard Pyle's romantic depiction of a galleon under attack conjures the menace that buccaneers posed to Spain's rich trade.

thousands of English, French, Spanish, Basque and Portuguese fishermen arrived every spring to harvest the seemingly endless fishing wealth of the banks, the shallow and productive waters between Nova Scotia and Newfoundland. Year-round settlement was discouraged and government was close to non-existent — a perfect recipe for piracy. Law was confined to the rule of the "Fishing Admirals," the first fishermen to arrive in the spring, who were given powers to settle disputes over fishing rights. The English Navy was in its infancy and confined to European waters.

In wartime, governments licensed privateers to attack their foreign fishing rivals, and in peacetime they turned a blind eye to those who continued, as pirates, to weaken their rivals. English officials in Newfoundland had a euphemistic but apt phrase for English privateers who turned pirates. They called them "erring captains." Many buccaneering captains also had special government commissions authorizing them to commandeer supplies and conscript sailors, supposedly for the defence of the colony. However these powers were a tempting invitation to extort supplies and drag men into piracy.

The losers of buccaneering battles in the North Atlantic could expect to lose all or part of their money and cargo, sometimes their ship, but rarely their lives. Buccaneers in the north seemed to prefer to keep the stakes low and usually "gave quarter," that is, they spared the lives of their

A depiction from 1615 of a French merchant ship fighting off Barbary Pirates.

captives. There are few accounts of wholesale massacre or torture, which was commonplace in the ruthless buccaneering struggles with the Spanish empire in the Caribbean. However it was piracy just the same, with voyages and often lives ruined at the whim of raiders answering to no one but themselves and their crews. One unfortunate English trader and captain, Richard Whitbourne, was captured by three different pirates in Newfoundland, as we will see.

Pirates were attracted to the rich fishing grounds off Newfoundland less for the money carried by large banks fishing vessels, which was modest, than for the ample supplies found aboard, and especially for the sailors themselves. This was an ideal hunting ground for manpower. More notoriously, the Barbary Pirates based in Algiers and Tunis in North Africa also raided the returning fishing fleets for slaves. Pirate vessels from all nations were to be found on the banks: French, Basque, Flemish, Spanish and Portuguese.

The king of pirates in this period, and probably the most successful pirate in Canadian history was Peter Easton. He is a grand example of a buccaneer who moved easily from legal privateer to outright pirate in this lawless era. Easton began as an English privateer, commissioned to attack Spanish vessels in the long series of wars between England and Spain in the late 1500s. However, in 1603, when England and Spain made peace, Easton continued to raid and became a pirate. His extensive attacks in the Bristol Channel in 1610 led the English crown to hire a privateer named Henry Mainwaring to stop him, but Easton left the Channel before Mainwaring arrived and avoided a direct confrontation. He first shifted his attention to West African waters before sailing to Newfoundland in 1612.

Easton was in his late thirties when he arrived in Newfoundland with four vessels led by his flagship *Happy Adventure*. His ships needed extensive work from their time in southern waters, so Easton selected Harbour Grace as a base. There he built a defensive battery, palisade and a modest house. He seized 100 men and the ship's carpenter from every ship in the area. Newfoundland had little government and virtually no record keeping, so reliable accounts of Easton's captures are hard to come by, but they were clearly substantial. He took 25 French ships, 12 Portuguese ships and one very large Flemish vessel worth £1,000. He plundered 30 English ships sheltered in St. John's Harbour. His total takings were estimated at more than £20,000. The captures added men and ships. His fleet grew to ten ships mounting 100 cannons, and estimates of the number of men at his command ran from 500 to 1,400.

Compared to the official English settlement struggling to establish itself at Cupids, not far from Harbour Grace, which mounted a mere three cannons and 40 settlers, Easton was clearly a law unto himself. However, except for one accidental attack that left one man wounded, he did not attack the Cupids settlers. Easton did not want to entirely cut his ties with England and sent enquiries there for a pardon. On the whole his attacks — described by the Governor at Cupids as "troublesome to the English and terrible to the French" — were felt most sharply by England's colonial rivals.

Easton did not confine his raids to the fishing fleets of Newfoundland. On July 17, 1711, he sailed south to attack Spanish ships and raid Puerto Rico. When he returned to Newfoundland, he found that armed fishermen from the Basque regions of Spain and France had occupied his base at Harbour Grace. The two small fleets clashed in a battle that saw considerable bloodshed. In the end, Easton prevailed, sinking many of the Basque ships. (Many accounts exaggerate the battle, suggesting that Easton wiped out an entire French naval squadron when, in fact, it was very much a frontier battle between two sets of private warriors.)

Easton captured English captain and merchant Richard Whitbourne in late 1611. Whitbourne found Easton "well furnished and very rich." Captive but comfortable, Whitbourne debated the merits of plunder with "the Arch Pyrate." Easton piled gold in front of the well-connected Whitbourne to sway him into piracy, while politely listening to Whitbourne's lectures about his "evil course." They struck a deal: Easton agreed he would return the ship of an English merchant he had captured in Africa if Whitbourne would sail it to England and seek a pardon. When Whitbourne arrived in England, he discovered that a pardon had already been issued for Easton.

While waiting for his pardon, Easton had assembled his ships in Ferryland for a large raid against the annual Spanish treasure fleet. Once a year, shipments of gold and silver from Spain's American colonies gathered together under naval protection to make the voyage to Spain. Easton successfully picked off four Spanish treasure ships.

By the time the pardon finally arrived from James I, Easton had wearied of the long wait, and in 1612 he dismissed it saying, "I am in a way a King myself." Easton then found a base with the Barbary Pirates in Tunis and a few years later with the Duke of Savoy in southern France.

Below: Mi'kmaq petro-glyph of an 18th century sloop.
Right: Mi'kmaq Encamp-ment, watercolour, 1791.

Distinguishing himself in several sieges he retired to the Duke's province, where he lived well. He married an heiress, built a warehouse for his wealth and retired from the sea in comfort.

The privateer who had originally been hired to put a stop to Easton's activities, Henry Mainwaring, instead followed his wake into piracy. At first he raided with the Barbary Pirates, attacking Spanish shipping near Gibraltar. On June 4, 1614, Mainwaring shifted his attention to Newfoundland. He sailed with six warships, captured two more on the Grand Banks and systemically raided the main harbours of Newfoundland. He left Newfoundland on September 14 with his holds full of supplies, some loot and his ships manned with 400 prime sailors from the fishing fleets — some volunteers, some forced.

Among those he captured was poor Richard Whitbourne, who had another season's voyage ruined. Mainwaring eventually released him to sail home for England, possibly sounding out the chance of a pardon.

Mainwaring returned to attacking Spanish ships with the Barbary Pirates until he was pardoned by James I in 1616. Returning to England, Mainwaring wrote one of the first histories of piracy in the North Atlantic, *The Beginnings, Practices and Suppression of Pirates*, in 1617. This privateer turned pirate finally became a naval admiral and retired as a knight.

Another buccaneer who cut a piratical swath through the region was Walter Raleigh. In 1618, as he was returning from a disastrous raid on the Orinoco River in South America, several of his ships raided French ships on the banks. They also robbed several English ships, including one belonging to the long-suffering Richard Whitbourne. But Raleigh was one buccaneer who took piracy too far. Spanish protests over his Orinoco expedition led to his execution by England's James I in 1619.

The English buccaneers did not confine their

raids to shipping. The Acadian settlements in Nova Scotia suffered many attacks from buccaneers like the brothers David and Lewis Kirke and Samuel Argall. Argall sailed up the coast from his colony in Virginia to attack Port Royal, Nova Scotia, in 1613. Despite the fact that England and France were at peace, Argall saw a chance to seize supplies and knock out a colonial rival.

French settlers were peacefully working their fields when they saw Argall's boats land and put their tiny unarmed fort to the torch. As England still claimed Nova Scotia, it gave Argall a thin excuse to loot

The reconstructed Port Royal Habitation and, above, a privateer cutlass blade.

and destroy the habitation built by Pierre De Monts and Samuel de Champlain. It was the first of many devastating raids on the Acadian settlements in the Bay of Fundy by the English colonies to the south.

Just as European powers promoted buccaneering as a tool of colonial expansion, some First Nations of the region also used sea power to defend their territorial goals. While Newfoundland's Beothuk withdrew into the interior for survival, the Mi'kmaq people of the region made assertive use of shipping raids to seek redress for grievances, re-enforce treaty demands and limit European expansion. Mi'kmaq raiders captured more than 80 ships along the coast from Massachusetts to Newfoundland prior to 1760.

The Mi'kmaq quickly adapted European nautical technology to their own uses, particularly the small single-masted boats called shallops. By 1630, it was common to see Mi'kmaq sailing shallops far from land, while their unique seagoing canoes remained supreme for portage travel. Sometimes Mi'kmaq attacks took place on a very large scale. In 1722, when war between natives and New Englanders in Maine spread to Nova Scotia, the Mi'kmaq seized 18 vessels in the Bay of Fundy and 18 more along the South Shore. They were seen cruising the coasts in their captured ships, using them as decoys to take even more New England vessels. The crew of an approaching English ship would think they were meeting just another fishing schooner until armed Mi'kmaq would leap up crying, "Strike English dogs, and come aboard, for you are all prisoners."

These attacks were inevitably referred to as "massacres" by Europeans. But although there were deaths, usually in the initial assault, the Mi'kmaq generally kept the crew prisoner to ransom or use as bargaining chips. Blood was shed, however, when the Mi'kmaq felt a need to take reprisals: a crew was killed in 1715, for example, following rumours that the English were deliberately poisoning Indian food, but such events were exceptions. Mi'kmaq ship attacks were, in this respect, no more bloodthirsty than other buccaneering attacks of the time.

The Mi'kmaq themselves repeatedly claimed that their seizures of vessels were statements of territorial control. On his release in 1715, a captured fishermen reported, "The Indians say ye lands are there and they can make war and peace when they please." Ships were seized to achieve immediate goals, such as the above-mentioned reprisals, forcing prisoner exchanges or stopping unwelcome traders — especially of alcohol. But the seizing of ships also had a broader goal of controlling Mi'kmaq territory. Mi'kmaq sea raids, combined with their land attacks, confined English settlements in Atlantic Canada to a handful of locations. The governor of Nova Scotia couldn't even complete a survey of potential settlement lands because his survey sloop was constantly being armed to chase after Mi'kmaq ship raiders. The Mi'kmaq would sustain their attacks at sea until 1760, when a lasting peace was finally negotiated with the British.

Unfortunately for the Mi'kmaq, what they saw as attacks to control their territory, the Europeans saw as piracy. Mi'kmaq vessels did not have commissions, Letters of Marque or letters from powerful royal patrons — the European trappings that distinguished a pirate from a buccaneer.

A telling comparison can be drawn between three Mi'kmaq who were captured after seizing a fishing schooner in 1726 and the notorious French privateer "Captain Baptiste" captured by the English a few years earlier. All had violently captured ships, although Baptiste had killed many more New Englanders than the Mi'kmaq prisoners had. The Mi'kmaq had a clear political agenda (an attempt to force an exchange of prisoners), but Baptiste had a piece of parchment showing he was serving the French state and was grudgingly accepted by the English as a privateer. Baptiste was released when the war ended. The Mi'kmaq were hanged.

The buccaneering era drew to a close in the late 1600s. The loosely regulated privateers and sometimes pirates who formed the buccaneering ranks had been useful in draining Spain's empire and carving out colonial claims. However, as their own empire grew, the British found that buccaneers could be a liability.

One man who embodied the changing times was William Kidd. The Scottish privateer rose to prominence in the freewheeling privateer warfare of the Caribbean in the 1680s. He briefly settled down in New York, where fate reached out to him in 1695. English pirates in the Indian Ocean were attacking the rich trade between India and the Red Sea, and a venture was hatched in London to send Kidd to capture the pirates and seize their treasure. The plan would, on paper, police the empire and enrich his investors at the same time. Kidd was outfitted with a custom-built pirate-hunting ship, the *Adventure Galley* and sent to the Indian Ocean.

He left England in April 1696, and in May he made the last legal capture of his career off Newfoundland. Kidd was sailing to New York to recruit crew in his hometown for the long voyage to India. He came upon a French fishing vessel, and since England and France were at war it was a legal, although not very rich, prize. However when Kidd finally reached his destination in the Indian Ocean, he began to hunt not pirates, but the rich ships of Indian and Arab merchants. These merchants were not at war with England.

Historians still debate whether Kidd's actions

William Kidd, the fantasy, a romantic depiction by Howard Pyle.

were due to greed or to a loss of control of his crew. His major capture was a large and richly laden Indian ship named the *Quedah Merchant*. Kidd reasoned that, like so many privateers who had turned pirate in the past, his plunder and success would buy a pardon and his attacks against neutrals and trading partners of the British would be overlooked. It had worked for Drake, Morgan, Easton and so many others.

Unfortunately for Kidd, the nature of trade and empire was changing. Wealthy British merchants were eager to cultivate regular trade and goodwill with the Indian and Arab merchants. They were not seeking plunder. Colonial governments now saw neutrals not just as targets but as trading partners. Warrants went out for Kidd's arrest, and despite his desperate attempts to bargain, using his remaining loot, he was shipped off to London for a quick and one-sided trial. He was hanged on May 23, 1701.

Kidd was not much of a pirate, but his highly publicized and very political trial marked an important turning point. As the eighteenth century dawned, aspiring swashbucklers would have to choose: pirate or privateer. They could either abide the increasingly regulated world of privateering with all kinds of restrictions on whom and how they could raid, or they could embrace true piracy and live with no controls or restrictions imposed by anyone. A captured pirate faced execution, but a captured privateer was treated as a prisoner of war.

As the buccaneering era came to an end in the late 1600s, governments dramatically tightened their controls on privateering. Laws were passed, and Vice Admiralty courts were set up all over the empire to regulate privateers. The Letter of Marque, the privateering license, became harder to obtain. Ship owners had to post a huge bond, up to £3,000, which they would lose if their captains misbehaved. The British Parliament even passed a law precisely defining the privateer's

flag. While pirates flew under the "Black Flag" of the Jolly Roger, privateers flew under the "Red Jack," a supersized union jack on a red background.

Privateering became a popular wartime activity as permanent settlements began to be established in Nova Scotia, with ships based at first in French settlements such as Port Royal and Louisbourg and later in English ports such as Halifax and especially Liverpool.

In a small port like Liverpool, merchants suffered the consequences of war in losses to the enemy, but did not see any of the benefits enjoyed by a garrison city like Halifax where the army and navy spent freely. Privateers from Liverpool scoured the Caribbean in the 1790s, raiding all the old French and Spanish trade routes previously attacked by the pirates. In the War of 1812, 50 privateers, licensed from every major port in Atlantic Canada, attacked

William Kidd, the reality, his corpse hanging in a gibbet.

American shipping, capturing more than 250 ships. One small Nova Scotian schooner alone, a former slave ship renamed the *Liverpool Packet*, took more than 50 American vessels.

A handful of Nova Scotian privateers did venture into piratical behaviour. In 1756, the crew of the privateer *Musketo* tortured captured sailors of a neutral ship to force them to reveal a hidden enemy cargo. The unfortunate Dutch sailors had thumbs screws applied to their limbs and genitals as the Halifax privateers danced them about the deck. However privateering was now firmly regulated, and the Dutch sailors were able to turn to the Halifax Vice Admiralty court for legal recourse. The owners of the *Musketo* had to return the cargo and pay compensation. Governments in Nova Scotia, New Brunswick and Newfoundland usually kept a tight control over their privateers to avoid such embarrassing incidents — and to ensure a government share of captures.

By the War of 1812, Nova Scotian privateers were more or less sticking to the rules. In fact,

they had a better reputation for respecting prisoners and property than did Britain's Royal Navy. American newspapers were full of accounts of brutal treatment and wanton destruction by what they called the "pirates" of the Royal Navy, who dragged American sailors to serve on British ships and seized cargoes with seemingly little cause. Complaints about the behaviour of privateers from British North America were virtually nonexistent.

The Americans themselves had embraced privateering with intense enthusiasm. The American Revolution in 1775 unleashed hordes of unlicensed American privateers. Not having Letters of Marque, nor being overseen by any court system, nor policed by a navy, they were legally pirates and many behaved as such. Their attacks went far beyond capturing vessels. They marched ashore, robbing houses, shops and farms to take money, shoe buckles and even glass from windowpanes. Their attacks against isolated Newfoundland fishing villages were often

A model of the wildly successful schooner Liverpool Packet.

A British merchant captain submits to a hard-faced boarding party from the relentless privateers of the American Revolution.

rebels. Many more had been neutral, but the relentless attacks forced people to take sides. Dozens of Newfoundland communities mounted cannons, many still visible today, to repel the Americans. Formerly pro-American ports like Liverpool made a remarkable transition, fighting off American attacks on their town and taking the war to the Americans with their own fleet of privateer schooners.

In an unintended fashion, the piratical attacks by the American privateers solidified support for the British and kept the region out of the new American republic. Later in the war, the new American government recognized the problem. George Washington issued decrees to control shore raids and the American government set up its own court system and licenses to bring privateers under control.

As government navies grew in size and political power during the nineteenth century, they discouraged most nations from private sector competition. Armoured warships with specialized modern weapons also became too expensive for most private investors. Privateering was eventually abolished in 1856 by an international treaty, the Declaration of Paris. However, a number of nations, including the United States, refused to sign it. To this day the power to grant privateering licenses remains in Article One of the United States Constitution.

devastating. They robbed communities of supplies on the brink of winter. Often they burned houses and even tiny fishing craft.

As the war continued, American privateer attacks grew even bolder. Whole towns were captured for a day so that the privateers could enjoy systematic, house-by-house looting. Lunenburg, Annapolis Royal, Saint John and Charlottetown were all sacked. These attacks fell hardest on ports where many had been sympathetic to the

BARTHOLOMEW ROBERTS AND THE GOLDEN AGE OF PIRACY

One cannot withhold admiration for his bravery and daring.

Samuel Shute, Governor of Massachusetts, 1720

The years from 1690 to 1730 saw the greatest outburst of piracy that the Atlantic has ever known. This is the period that generated the images and legends that dominate our perception of piracy today. Almost all the household names of piracy come from this period: Blackbeard, Calico Jack, Anne Bonny, Black Bart and Captain Kidd. Historians writing long after these menacing figures were safely dead were so impressed by the scale and vivid characters in this time that they coined the grandiose but useful title "the Golden Age of Piracy."

The pirates of this era drew inspiration and customs from the earlier buccaneers, but they dropped the pretence of robbing for king or country. They robbed all nations to live as they pleased. Many cultivated colourful personal images of terror and defiance. During these four short decades, more than 5,000 pirates aboard hundreds of ships were lurking in the North Atlantic Ocean. At times they brought trade to a standstill, terrified colonial mariners and made even colonial governors fear for their lives. In this period, pirates captured more English ships than the combined fleets of Spain and France had managed to take from 1701 to 1714, during

By 1716, the life of a sailor was bleak and the life of a pirate was tempting.

the War of the Spanish Succession.

Piracy exploded during these years for a number of reasons. Several generations of men had embraced the easy discipline and rich rewards of buccaneering and were reluctant to abandon it just because London would no longer turn a blind eye to piracy. And while the home government was eager to crack down on piracy, many poor and corrupt colonies were willing to be more accommodating. But the biggest contributor was the abrupt end in 1714 to the War of the Spanish Succession. By 1717, the British navy had slashed its manpower from a wartime peak of almost 54,000 to just over 6,000. Licenses for privateers expired as soon as peace was declared, throwing thousands more out of work. Wages were slashed, too. A vessel from the West Indies that had paid wartime wages of £4 a month in 1714 arrived in Lisbon and hired a new crew at a mere £1.15 a month.

Conditions for seamen grew worse as trade slumped by 1715. Many merchants and owners safeguarded their profits by, in the words of the sailors themselves, "using their men severely." They drove their men hard, cheated them of wages and shortchanged their rations. The life of a sailor, always hard and dangerous, was now bleak, grinding and often hopeless. It is little wonder that many chose piracy, because they had nothing to lose. Even a small crew of pirates found that they could quickly multiply — with every ship they took many captives joined them. Even those forced to join the pirates often found that the freedom and money were addictive, staying until the gallows found them.

As the motivation for piracy peaked, so did the opportunities. Sailors knew that much rich trade was poorly protected. The peacetime navy was small and inclined to remain in port. Naval captains were often reluctant to chase pirates, slow fuses, wreathing his head in a sulphureous haze. While his look was monstrous, his treatment of prisoners was merciful.

Blackbeard rarely killed anyone, succeeding by fear alone and quickly releasing his captured ships. For a time he seemed unstoppable, blockading Charleston, South Carolina and — at least according to legend — fighting off a 30-gun British naval frigate. Blackbeard's end came on November 17, 1718, in a close-fought battle with two naval sloops. He went down fighting, shot five times. The naval sloop returned to port with his head mounted on its bowsprit.

The piracy of this period is usually most closely associated with the Caribbean; indeed the terms "pirates" and "Caribbean" have become inseparably intertwined. In some ways it is a well deserved reputation. The great pirate historian Charles Johnson wrote in 1724, "Pyrates infest the West Indies they are more numerous than any other parts of the World." He pointed to the many uninhabited islands where pirates could hide, hunt for food and repair their vessels in safety and comfort.

preferring to earn fees for escorting rich ships or carrying private cargoes. For a number of years pirates faced little chance of capture.

A man named Edward Teach, forever after known as Blackbeard, was one of those who knew just how ripe the time was for piracy. Thrown on hard times at the war's end, he turned pirate in 1716. He quickly built up a crew of unhappy seamen aboard his large ship, the *Queen Anne's Revenge*. He cultivated a fierce reputation among his own men and victims with his enormous black beard in which he would burn

Captain Edward Teach - "Blackbeard"

A modern depiction of Blackbeard's ferocious final moments in battle with the British Navy.

However there were in fact four major destinations for pirate raids and bases in this period. Apart from the Caribbean, a second, formative area was the Indian Ocean with its rich trade between the Red Sea and India and safe bases on the island of Madagascar, off the southeast coast of Africa. It was a region that proved an important breeding ground for pirates at the beginning of the Golden Age, and also for the undoing of erstwhile pirate hunter William Kidd.

A third major area was the West Coast of Africa. The massive profits of the slave trade attracted ships laden with gold and expensive goods to ports like Whydah, today known as Ouidah, in Benin, "that port where commonly is the best booty," in Charles Johnson's words. Many pirate ships originated from mutinies on slave ships in West Africa and it was here — where piracy threatened the inhumane, but profitable transatlantic slave trade — that the Royal Navy would most decisively concentrate its efforts to crush piracy.

The fourth — and often overlooked — destination for pirates during the Golden Age was the region known today as Atlantic Canada, comprising the provinces of Nova Scotia, New Brunswick, Prince Edward Island and especially Newfoundland. Henry Mainwaring had noted its growing popularity with pirates in the 1600s: "They easily get bread, wine, cider, and fish enough, with all necessities from shipping. In Newfoundland, if they be of good force, they will command all the land in regard as the fishermen will not stand with each other."

In 1724, Charles Johnson wrote that Newfoundland attracted pirates because of its many secure harbours plus the greed of fishing merchants whose indentured servitude and low wages left men "not be able to subsist themselves, they sometimes run away with shallops and boats and begin pyratical Exploits. And secondly they are visited almost every summer by some set of Pyrates already raised who lay in for a store of water and provisions."

European powers called the Newfoundland fishery "the nursery of seamen" because it trained so many potential sailors for their navies. Pirates found that the fishery served the same purpose for them. Newfoundland harbours and their offshore fishing fleets provided probably the richest source of crews for pirates of the Golden Age. Although the amount of gold on fishing ships was modest, the fishing banks off Newfoundland and Nova Scotia were also rich in transatlantic merchant ships carrying valuable cargoes and sometimes wealthy passengers. Another large fishery was based in Cape Breton, where the French were just beginning to build the fortress of Louisbourg.

The tiny population and weak colonial authorities in Atlantic Canada were certainly no threat to the pirates. Newfoundland had a growing but widely scattered series of fishing settlements, but no real government beyond the seasonal administration of two Royal Navy ships stationed in St. John's. In Nova Scotia, New Brunswick and Prince Edward Island, small Acadian agricultural settlements tried to stay out of European conflicts, while the Mi'kmaq fought to contain the small encircled British garrison at

Left: The fishing banks off Atlantic Canada drew both fishermen and pirates.
Below: Newfoundland's many sheltered and isolated harbours attracted pirates.

Annapolis Royal. The province's countless harbours remained mostly unsettled and provided fine hiding places. A growing fleet of fishing vessels from New England maintained a settlement at Canso on the eastern shore of Nova Scotia and also used seasonal harbours around Cape Sable at the extreme southwest tip of Nova Scotia.

The most successful pirate of this age was Bartholomew Roberts. While politics made William Kidd legendary and a ferocious image made Blackbeard famous, Roberts took more ships than both put together. His raids brought trade to a standstill in the Caribbean on numerous occasions. He was a fearless and bold pirate tactician. He was also an effective, although sometimes ruthless, leader of his independent and fearless followers. Lesser pirates couldn't attract crews or find prizes, or they grew careless or cowardly enough to be captured. Roberts died in battle at the height of his success, as he always boasted he would.

He was selective in his violence, most often releasing his victims after robbing them, but he did not hesitate to be ruthless. He oversaw trials of his own men, who were shot for desertion, and he permitted torture of some captives to force them to reveal hidden cargo. Roberts' cruellest act was the savage murder of 80 slaves, when he burned a slave ship whose captain refused to pay ransom: his men could not be bothered to unshackle those aboard. Although he could respect captains who tried to defend their ships, Roberts nursed a bitter hatred towards shore authorities who insulted him or tried to capture him.

Roberts was one of the few pirates who dressed lavishly. Eyewitnesses at his last battle described him as "dressed in a rich crimson damask waistcoat and breeches, a red feather in his hat, a gold chain round his neck, with a diamond cross hanging to it, a sword in his hand, and two pairs of pistols slung over his shoulders." He had a taste for showmanship, flying very expressive flags and

firing off salutes. He employed scores of musicians who played six days a week for the crew's pleasure and to terrify the opposition in battle with pounding drums. Playing for Roberts' music-loving pirates was demanding. Four musicians who escaped from him in 1722 told authorities that they had "an uneasy life of it, having sometime their Fiddles and often their Heads broke only for excusing themselves or saying they were tired."

He lived up to all the bold images of a pirate captain, but in some ways he was exceptional. He seldom drank and he was religious. He once tried to persuade a captured clergyman to join his crew to preach Sunday sermons. The minister declined and Roberts released him, but stole the minister's prayer books for his own reflection and the

Right: Swivel gun that defended the French treasure ship Chameau *against pirates.*
Below: A pirate steals away from a town that strongly suggests Louisbourg.

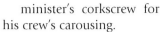

minister's corkscrew for his crew's carousing.

Roberts' pirate career began in 1719. He was 37, older than most pirates, and an officer aboard a slave ship captured in West Africa by the pirate Howell Davis. Despite being forced to join, Roberts took to piracy with enthusiasm. When Davis was killed in an ambush at a Portuguese slave-trading settlement on the island of Principe in West Africa, Roberts was elected captain. He declared, philosophically, "that since he had dipp'd his Hands in Muddy Water, and must be a Pyrate, it was better being a Commander than a common Man."

His first act was to burn the Portuguese settlement and its shipping in a bloody act of revenge. He next led his men across the Atlantic to spectacular success in Brazil, attacking large convoys, intimidating Portuguese warships and scouring the West Indies. His raids choked off colonial trade in parts of the Caribbean altogether. Roberts' crew and ships grew in number and some would

then often split off from his pirate squadrons to pursue their own nefarious ways. The governors of Barbados and Martinique hired armed ships to hunt him down, but he escaped to nurse deep grudges against both islands. As resistance was stiffening in the Caribbean, Roberts set Atlantic Canada in his sights and sailed north in the spring of 1720.

His first landfall was Canso, where he set about robbing ships of the New England fishing fleet. Next he crossed the Gulf of Saint Lawrence and captured an English merchant ship and three French fishing vessels. From the English ship he forced an officer named Moses Renos to join his crew for the next six months. Roberts decided his ships needed a refit and selected Trepassey, a growing but undefended fishing harbour south of St. John's.

His bellicose arrival, with drums beating, trumpets blaring, black flags flying and cannons firing, had exactly the effect he wanted. Rumours had already arrived about his captures off Nova Scotia, which generated the fear that was Roberts' most effective weapon. He met no resistance and all the ships of the harbour were abandoned. Roberts stayed in Trepassey for two weeks. He summoned the captains of all 22 captured ships to daily meetings, demanding men and supplies and threatening to burn the ship of any captain who did not attend.

Accounts of his occupation are vivid, but differ in the extent of the destruction he wreaked. Boston newspapers and historian Charles Johnson painted a picture of wanton devastation. They blamed Roberts for destroying wharves, warehouses and sheds. "It is impossible particularly to recount the Destruction and Havoc they made here, burning and sinking all the shipping, except a Bristol Galley, and destroying the Fisheries and the Stages [wharves] of the poor Planters without remorse or compunction."

However the one eyewitness who wrote down

Above: Bartholomew Roberts, his ships and captured prizes at the height of his success in Africa, 1722.
Left: A pirate re-enactor tries to match Roberts' swagger and lavish dress.

what he saw, Moses Renos, said that Roberts burned only a single ship, paid local carpenters for their work and bought — not stole — cannons and supplies from ashore. Rich with looted currency, Roberts could buy unlimited amounts of willing work in a cash-starved economy from fishermen used to pitiful wages. Discontented fishermen and merchant sailors joined his crew,

along with some forced men whose skills Roberts sought. The volunteers included a fisherman named Thomas How, who would follow the pirate to the very end.

It would not have been difficult to send word overland to the British garrison at Placentia and summon the Royal Navy's station ship, but no one did, possibly because the pirate's business

was welcome. Roberts took his time looting the ships at anchor and waited in leisure as four more merchant ships arrived to be robbed in turn. One impressive vessel that caught his eye was the *Bristol Galley*, a large ship fitted with oar ports that could be rowed in calm seas. Roberts mounted 16 guns in the *Galley* and made her his flagship under the name *Royal Fortune*.

Subjecting Trepassey to a final bombardment as they left, the two ships *Fortune* and *Royal Fortune* sailed north to Cape Spear, looting fishing vessels along the way. One ship they took on the coast of Newfoundland was the *Blessing*. On board the pirates spotted a massive 20-year-old sailor named John Walden whom they forced to join them. Walden was soon nicknamed "Miss Nanny," in jest at his tough demeanour. Respected for his great strength he became, in the words of his shipmates, "a staunch Pyrate and great Rouge" who would fight with Roberts to the final battle. He could lift anchors and cut mooring cables with one blow and was usually sent aboard captured ships with a poleaxe as the "key" to smash open locked doors and chests in search of loot.

Roberts' foray at Trepassey sent shock waves throughout northeastern North America. The French Governor at Louisbourg, St. Ovide de Brouillant, was struggling to construct the massive fortress and sent warnings to France about his vulnerability to pirate attack. He had, on paper, a garrison of about 300, but many of his

soldiers were so unreliable they regularly sold their muskets. Worse, there was often no powder or shot for the measly six guns mounted to defend the town.

St. Ovide was right to be worried. Roberts was heading right for him. After *Royal Fortune* and *Fortune* had finished their short cruise to Cape Spear they steered for Cape Breton, where the French overseas fishery had its largest base. The two pirate ships caught 10 French fishing vessels. Roberts and his men were harsh on their French victims, burning each ship and torturing some crew. Their last French capture was a large merchant ship of 26 guns that the pirates decided to keep, making her the new *Royal Fortune* and abandoning the former *Bristol Galley* to their assembled French prisoners to make their way home. Two sloops were renamed *Great Ranger* and *Little Ranger*. In a few weeks Roberts' command had grown from one sloop with 45 men and 10 guns to a small fleet with several hundred men.

Roberts, however, passed up the opportunity to raid Louisbourg. A defended royal harbour — even a poorly defended one — would be a costly prize. Much more rewarding for his newly expanded squadron were the busy shipping lanes running through Atlantic Canada. The pirate squadron headed out to the Grand Banks to intercept the main trade between North America and England. Roberts used *Little Ranger* as the scout, and a string of merchant ships easily fell into his hands: *Richard*, *Willing Mind* and *Expectation*.

As *Samuel*'s master, Captain Cary, watched this wanton waste, the pirates boasted to him that they feared no one and would seek no pardon: "King and Parliament might be damned with their Acts of Clemency for them; neither would they be hang'd up a sun as Kid's company were but if they should ever be overpower'd, they would set Fire to the Powder with a Pistol and all go merrily to Hell together." After hauling

£8,000 of plunder from the ship, the pirates were debating whether to burn or scuttle the *Samuel,* when the ship was saved by the appearance of another sail on the horizon. The pirates released the looted ship to give chase to another victim. That vessel belonged to Captain Bowles from Bristol who unfortunately shared the same hometown as the hated governor of Barbados, which earned him a vicious beating.

The Grand Banks had given Roberts' men a rich haul, but it wasn't over yet. A final string of vessels was robbed and then released: *Little York* and *Love* on July 16, and *Phoenix* and *Sadbury* the following day. A final capture was a brigantine whose crew was taken aboard the *Royal Fortune* to watch their vessel sink in flames.

Now rich in plunder and manpower, but low on supplies, Roberts finally left the waters of Atlantic Canada and took his pirate squadron back to the Caribbean for the rest of the year. In southern waters his bold success in seeking booty and vengeance continued. He now flew a flag with an image of himself standing on two skulls labelled "A Barbadian's Head" and "A Martinican's Head." Roberts made capture after capture, issuing threats, challenges and ultimatums to governors everywhere he went. One of his many captures was a French ship that happened to be carrying the Governor of Martinique. With cruel satisfaction, Roberts promptly hanged the Governor from the yardarm of his own ship.

Making another bold move into new waters,

Tools of the gunner's trade including round shot, canister shot and a bagged cartridge of grapeshot, the multiple balls of iron that killed Bartholomew Roberts.

Roberts took his fleet to West Africa in the spring of 1721. For months, they raided the many slave ports of the coast and the gold-laden ships that came to buy slaves. The end for Roberts finally came on February 10, 1722, when HMS *Swallow,* after months of searching, caught up with his fleet.

The great pirate was killed at the very beginning of the battle, his throat ripped open by grapeshot as he leapt onto a gun carriage to direct his return fire. Complying with his long-standing request, the pirates quickly threw his body overboard wearing all his finery, so that his body would never hang in a gibbet. Demoralized and drunk, Roberts' men put up a weak fight, but his old Newfoundland hand, John Walden ("Miss Nanny"), was one of the few who fought on until a naval shot took off his leg.

Naval gunfire sent *Royal Fortune*'s mast crashing down with Roberts' final flag, a skeleton and a man holding a flaming sword. His crew surrendered soon after. About 250 pirates survived the

HMS Swallow *finally catches the* Royal Fortune *in 1722 as Bartholomew Roberts goes down fighting.*

battle to be taken in chains to Cape Coast Castle in present day Ghana. Many died awaiting trial, but 74 were acquitted and 54 were sentenced to death for piracy. Many were unrepentant, especially those of his crew who had been with him since the beginning. They called themselves "The House of Lords" and one, Thomas Sutton, nicknamed "Lord Sutton," mocked those seeking redemption. "Heaven! You fool! Did you ever hear of a pirate going thither. Give me hell. It is a merrier place. I'll give Roberts a salute of 13 guns at the entrance." Thomas How, who had joined Roberts back in Trepassey, dodged the hangman, but was sentenced to seven years service with the Royal African Company, a fate few survived. In spite of the bleeding stump of his leg, John Walden went to the hangman undaunted.

The scale of Roberts' operation made him unique. He had taken more than 400 ships, 55 of them off Nova Scotia and Newfoundland. His extravagant personal style of dress, fondness for music, flags and merry living matched up to everything people wanted to believe about pirates. Ending his career was a triumph for the Royal Navy and marked the turning point in the war against the pirates of the Golden Age. Never again would squadrons of pirate ships scour the Atlantic. From Barbados to Martinique, from Louisburg to Trepassey, merchants heaved a sigh of relief. Famous in his time, Roberts became a legend after his death, acquiring the posthumous nickname "Black Bart."

LOATHSOME NED LOW

If ever a man sailing the seas deserved to be hanged and gibbeted in chains, it was Low. If one half the tales that are told about him are true, he must have been at times a little short of maniac.

George Francis Dow, *Pirates of the New England Coast*

Next to Bartholomew Roberts, the pirate most strongly connected to Atlantic Canada was also one of the most vicious: Edward (Ned) Low. While many pirates of this period were respected for their courage in battle or mercy to captives, Low had no redeeming qualities. He was known for unpredictable rages, torture and cowardice. One minute he would seem meek and ingratiating, the next he would shoot people in the head or burn them alive.

Low started bad and ended worse. He was born in Westminster, where he learned extortion as a child. As a teenager he ran a crooked gambling ring for footmen in the lobby of the House of Commons. Low emigrated to Boston, married and turned honest for a time, working as a ship rigger. But his business struggled, and he grew to hate the shipowners and captains of New England. His wife died and then his son, leaving only his daughter. In 1722, at the age of 32, Low signed on a log-cutting voyage to Honduras. He quarrelled with the captain and took a shot at the man before making off with a small boat and a few companions, determined "to go in her, make a Black Flag and declare War against all the World."

He started with 13 followers. They soon joined forces with George Lowther aboard the brigantine *Happy Delivery*, who had turned pirate

in a slave-ship mutiny in Africa. After making a dozen captures and surviving an attack by natives at Port Mayo, where *Happy Delivery* was lost, the surviving crew voted on May 28, 1722, to part company. Low and 44 men took the newly captured brigantine *Rebecca*, while Lowther sailed away with an equal number of men in the sloop *Ranger*.

Lowther led an eventful career, including a cruise in June and July of 1723 to the Grand Banks, where he and his men took several vessels and raided Newfoundland harbours. However, in October 1723, he was trapped by a determined armed sloop from Barbados while repairing his ship on an island off Venezuela. Most of his men were captured or deserted and Lowther committed suicide rather than face capture.

Low evidently still nursed a hatred of New Englanders over his failed business in Boston and picked as his target one of the wealthier colonies in the American northeast, Rhode Island. He robbed two vessels close to Rhode Island, but the captain of one, despite being deliberately wounded by Low to prevent him from raising the alarm, managed to get ashore and alert the authorities. The Governor of Rhode Island quickly called up volunteers and sent out an armed sloop that sighted and almost caught Low. Boston mustered another 100 men to take up the chase. The pirate narrowly escaped. Lacking supplies and water to return to the Caribbean, his men chose instead to attack one of the New England fishing bases in Nova Scotia.

So it was that Shelburne, Nova Scotia, then known as Port Roseway, became the place where Low carried out his first spectacular raid. Near

the southwest tip of Nova Scotia, Port Roseway was unsettled, but its large and easily approached harbour often sheltered visiting New England fishing vessels. On the sleepy morning of June 15, 1723, a mysterious brigantine appeared in the outer harbour of Port Roseway, where 13 large fishing vessels of the New England fishing fleet lay sheltered at anchor. The brigantine sailed between the anchored fishing vessels and quickly disgorged a boatload of heavily armed men. They hoisted to the masthead a chilling black flag showing a skeleton stabbing a bleeding heart. Low himself thundered to everyone within range that all would die if any resisted.

The fishermen collectively outnumbered Low by a wide margin. A number of their fishing schooners were larger than Low's brigantine

Charles Brooking captures the mood of the peaceful Sunday of the New England fishing fleet at Port Roseway just before it was shattered by Low's raid.

Rebecca. While none was heavily armed, between them they mounted more guns than the two cannons and four swivel guns aboard *Rebecca*. The pirate and his 44 men were also outnumbered by hundreds of fishermen. However the black flag and Low's brutal promise so terrified the fishing captains that none dared resist or even try to cut their anchor cables and escape. Over the next three days Low's men looted each ship at leisure, took whatever they wanted and looked over each crew for potential recruits. Low even had time to put his favourite dog ashore to roam free from wooden decks.

To make their job easier, the pirates beached

Above: Cliffs at the harbour entrance in St. John's.
Right: As the fog lifted, a large ship was revealed at anchor in St. John's.
Left: Low did much of his recruiting with a pistol such as this 18th century turnoff pistol.

forced, at pistol point, some of the more experienced and skilled fishermen to join.

Low chose the *Mary*, a large new fishing schooner from Marblehead, as his new ship. He renamed her *Fancy* and used forced labour provided by the fishermen to convert her to a pirate ship by mounting ten guns taken from the other fishing vessels. The pirate schooner born that day in Shelburne Harbour would serve Low long and hard. He repeatedly took and discarded other larger vessels, but *Fancy* was with him the longest, surviving battles and hurricanes and witnessing much blood on her decks. The pirates put the fishermen who wouldn't join them aboard their old brigantine *Rebecca*, and ordered the ship to sail to Boston.

Howls from the shoreline reminded the pirates to bring Low's dog aboard, which allowed two of the forced men to escape on shore. A third,

one schooner to use as a makeshift prison, cramming most of the fishermen from the other vessels into its hold under guard so there would be no danger of resistance or escape. The pirates first called for volunteers and then used an escalating series of threats and inducements to persuade the fishermen to sign up. Some men discovered that being married got them off the hook. One of Low's few scruples, shared with a number of pirates, was not to take married men, finding that those with no ties to home made better pirates. A surprising number joined Low, nearly doubling his numbers to 80. In the end the pirates also

Philip Ashton, tried to join them but was caught by the pirate quartermaster. The furious pirate put his pistol to Ashton's head and pulled the trigger. Nothing happened. The pistol misfired three times and the quartermaster finally threw it overboard in frustration. Ashton would survive for months aboard Low's ship, providing an eyewitness account of the wrathful man. As *Fancy* escorted *Rebecca* out of Shelburne Harbour on the afternoon of June 19, the fishermen looked back with dismay at the sight of their ravaged and abandoned schooners but counted themselves lucky that no one had been killed.

As Low set sail for Newfoundland, Ashton, a religious man, was both terrified and offended by life aboard. "I soon found that any Death was preferable to being link'd with such a vile Crew of Miscreants, to whom it was a sport to do mischief; where prodigious Drinking, monstrous Cursing and Swearing, hideous Blasphemies, and the open defiance of Heaven and contempt of Hell was the constant employment."

Fancy arrived at the mouth of St. John's Harbour on July 2 in thick fog. The mist lifted enough to reveal, through the narrows, a large ship with a row of gun ports at anchor in the harbour. Low guessed her to be a sack ship, one of the large merchant ships sent to Newfoundland to trade for and transport fish to Europe. Although clearly armed, she would have money aboard for trading and would make a rich prize. Low resolved to take her by deception. He ordered his men and their weapons hidden below, hoping *Fancy* would be mistaken for a fishing schooner until she was close enough for the crew to swarm aboard their victim.

However, as Low approached the narrows, he was hailed by an outbound fishing boat. To the shock and consternation of the pirates, they learned that their intended target was in fact HMS *Solebay*, a 24-gun ship of the Royal Navy, stationed in Newfoundland to protect the fisheries. Low instantly saw the long odds of taking on the disciplined crew of a warship and quickly put about, heading north to find a more vulnerable harbour to attack.

He settled on Carbonear, just to the west of St. John's in Conception Bay, not far from Peter Easton's old headquarters at Harbour Grace. He found no substantial shipping there so his men contented themselves with plundering homes and burning those whose welcome displeased them. Low's next target was the Grand Banks, where he took seven vessels. Several were French, and they provided a vast quantity of wine. Months later Low's men were still talking about the fine French claret.

One of the French captures was a fishing ship from St. Malo heading to Cape Breton. After Low had picked over their fishing supplies, he broke

The gun batteries of Fortress Louisbourg, including the Island Battery on the far left, first armed to defend Louisbourg against pirates.

yards, slashed rigging and told the ship to return to France. The French captain instead limped to Scaterie on Cape Breton and sent word to warn Louisbourg of the pirate schooner. Louisbourg had also been cautioned by the English Governor at Annapolis Royal, who sent a courtesy warning after he got word of Low's raid on Port Roseway. The threat of pirate attack led the acting French Governor, François Le Coutre de Bourville, to hurriedly erect gun batteries — 13 cannons on the mainland and seven heavy 24-pounders on the island guarding the entrance to the harbour. This was the beginning of Fortress Louisbourg's essential "Island Battery," which would play a critical role in the famous sieges of 1746 and 1758, but which, in fact, began as a defence against pirates.

Low made one more capture on the Grand Banks, a very large French fishing ship known as a banker, with two guns. He put Charles Harris

in charge of the captured French ship. Harris had been forced to join the pirates from a captured ship in the Caribbean, but had now taken to piracy with enthusiasm. From the French the pirates learned that HMS *Solebay* was hunting for them, so Low, now boasting two ships and more than 100 men, left Newfoundland to see what he could find in Canso, Nova Scotia.

Low arrived at the Canso landfall well ahead of Harris in the French banker. He spotted two heavily laden merchant sloops outbound from the harbour and gave chase. They proved to be taking provisions from Canso to Annapolis Royal for the garrison at Fort Anne. Unfortunately for Low, they included a small contingent of soldiers who repelled Low's schooner with disciplined volleys of musket fire. Never known for boldness in battle, Low hung back, waiting for the French banker to join him. However by the time the slow banker arrived, the

Low's ships narrowly escaped destruction as they fled south before a hurricane, much as these fishing sloops flee an approaching storm.

sloops had pulled away. Low's two ships gave chase, driving southwest along the Nova Scotian coast for two days in a cat-and-mouse game. Near Cape Sable the sloops were able to escape into a fog bank and Low lost them.

With Nova Scotia and Newfoundland now on the alert, the pirates decided to sail for new quarry in the Caribbean. However, Atlantic Canada had one more test for them. An early season hurricane hit just as the two ships began their voyage south. Both were soon fighting for survival amid mountainous waves and howling winds. The banker had the worst of it, wallowing in the waves and taking on enormous amounts of water. As water rose in the hold the pumps were constantly manned and augmented by bucket brigades. The pirates threw overboard six of their precious cannons, many of their provisions and some of their heavier loot.

Low's two ships crawled south and put into a small island in the Windward Caribbean for repairs. After robbing a helpless ship dismasted by the hurricane, Low's crew held a vote to decide on their next move. They chose to sail east to attack shipping in the mid-Atlantic Azores. In the months that followed the pirates enjoyed spectacular success, taking ship after ship. They pulled off bold night raids on harbours and forced governors to provide water and supplies by holding ships hostage.

Above: Facing capture by Ned Low, the desperate captain of Nostre Signora de Victoria *cuts loose a fortune in gold.*
Right: Ned Low's vile temper is a challenge for even the most over-the-top pirate re-enactors to capture.

However, in the Azores Low seems to have snapped. Until this time, he had more or less followed the usual pirate custom of "rob and release," occasionally burning the ships of those he disliked, but rarely harming crew or passengers. But now he and his men began to torture their victims. It began hideously in early August of 1722, when Low decided to burn a large French ship. As usual, the pirates let the crew go, except for the cook, whom they decreed "being a greasy Fellow would fry well in the Fire." He was tied to the mainmast and burned alive with the ship.

Low and his men took their cruelties to a new level on August 20, 1723. They captured an English vessel, the *Wright Galley*. The men went on a rampage, witnessed by the English captain. They chased their prisoners about the deck and slashed and hacked randomly, wounded many and killing several. Not liking the sorrowful expression of one helpless Portuguese passenger, one of Low's men disembowelled him. The brutality culminated in the hanging of two Franciscan friars from the foremast, the pirates hauling them into the air and dropping them to the deck several times to prolong the execution.

The madness caught up with Low when one of his own men misdirected a slash at a prisoner and accidently sliced Low's face. The surgeon, "tolerably drunk as it was the custom of everyone to be," quickly stitched up the injury but when Low complained of his rough work, the man punched Low in the face, ripping his stitches out and declared, "Bid him sew up his chops himself and be damned." The incident left Low with a hideously scarred facial expression.

A few months later Low, still sailing the schooner *Fancy*, captured a rich Portuguese ship, the *Nostre Signora de Victoria*. Several men were tortured to reveal where money was hidden. They confessed that once the pirates had been sighted, the captain had suspended a bag of gold coins, worth thousands of pounds, from the stern window and had cut it loose into the sea when they were taken. Low went berserk at this news and inflicted what became his trademark torture. He ordered the captain's lips be cut off

and cooked in front of him. He then had the captain and all 32 of the crew killed.

In March 1723, Low's men massacred another entire crew, this time of a Spanish privateer that had captured some English logwood smugglers. Low's use of torture against anyone who caught his attention was now common although unpredictable. Ships were still mostly robbed and released, but

Low made a point of slicing up the nose and cutting off the ears of any captain from New England. Others had their fingers burned to the bone by lit fuses that were tied to their hands.

While they were on the coast of Honduras, Philip Ashton, one of the fishermen forced aboard back in Shelburne, decided he was better off in the jungle than aboard Low's floating hell. He ran off during a watering party and survived a year as a castaway before being rescued.

To cruelty Low added cowardice on March 10, 1723, when he fell into a trap laid by the Royal Navy. Low had replaced his old Shelburne schooner with a newly captured sloop also named *Fancy*. He was sailing together with the sloop *Ranger* in the charge of his second-in-command, Charles Harris. The two pirates sighted what they thought was a large merchant ship. It was in fact a British naval frigate, HMS *Greyhound* searching for Low.

Peter Solgard, *Greyhound*'s British commander, prolonged the deception until the two pirate sloops drew within musket range and hoisted their pirate colours. Up went *Greyhound*'s naval colours and Solgard opened fire. It was a fierce two-hour battle. As the shooting started, the pirates hoisted red flags to show they would take no prisoners. *Greyhound* was a relatively small 20-gun warship, outnumbered by the two manoeuvrable sloops. However at a crucial moment naval gunfire brought the main yard crashing down aboard Harris's sloop. Low decided to sacrifice Harris and fled. Abandoned by Low, with 10 men dead, Harris surrendered. He went to the gallows with 34 of his men at Rhode Island, although another 10 convinced the court that they were forced men and were spared.

Humiliated and on the run, Low turned

❸ *Model of Ned Low's pirate sloop* Ranger, *typical of the small but fast and heavily armed sloops favoured by pirates.*

A Dutch marine painting evoking the flight of the small sloop from Canso pursued by Low's two large pirate ships.

towards Atlantic Canada, but he first paused to take prizes and revenge on New England. He took a series of small whaling sloops off Rhode Island. Their captains were tortured one after another. Low had one stripped naked and whipped, then he cut off the man's ears and shot him in the head. One was beheaded and another was disembowelled. He chopped the ears off one man, seasoned them with salt and pepper and forced his victim to eat them. Low's behaviour was growing so grotesque that even his own bloodthirsty crew developed misgivings and refused to carry out some of his more diabolical orders.

Now at his worst, Low turned to Nova Scotia. Mercifully, Shelburne was spared another visit. Instead, Low scoured the coasts of Cape Breton. He took a few fishing vessels from Canso, and his cruelty to English victims seemed to moder-

ate. His major captures, however, were 23 French fishing vessels off Cape Breton. The pirates kept one of them, a large armed ship of 22 guns, which was manned as a companion vessel to replace the sloop of the late Captain Harris. A fisherman in Canso writing to Boston noted how "Low uses the English very kindly but the French find little Mercy at his hand; they cut off some of their ears and noses and treated them with all the Barbarity Imaginable."

One French captain made the tragic mistake of asking Low for a receipt for his looted cargo of wine and brandy. (Bartholomew Roberts would proudly issue receipts for his captures.) Low fired one pistol into the man's stomach saying, "this is for your wine," and fired another into his head saying, "this is for your brandy."

HMS *Greyhound* came north with HMS *Seahorse* and searched fruitlessly for Low for

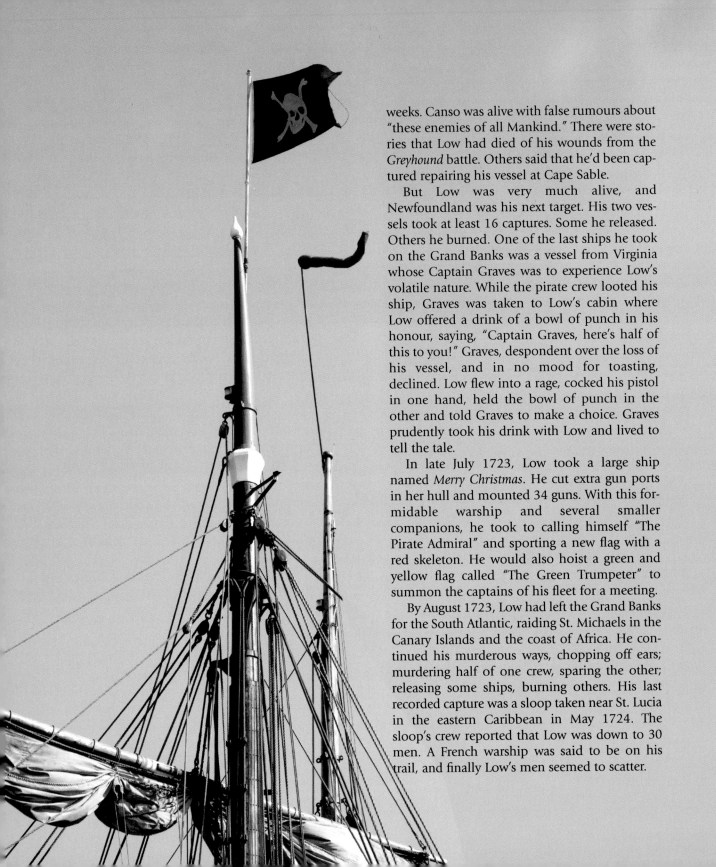

weeks. Canso was alive with false rumours about "these enemies of all Mankind." There were stories that Low had died of his wounds from the *Greyhound* battle. Others said that he'd been captured repairing his vessel at Cape Sable.

But Low was very much alive, and Newfoundland was his next target. His two vessels took at least 16 captures. Some he released. Others he burned. One of the last ships he took on the Grand Banks was a vessel from Virginia whose Captain Graves was to experience Low's volatile nature. While the pirate crew looted his ship, Graves was taken to Low's cabin where Low offered a drink of a bowl of punch in his honour, saying, "Captain Graves, here's half of this to you!" Graves, despondent over the loss of his vessel, and in no mood for toasting, declined. Low flew into a rage, cocked his pistol in one hand, held the bowl of punch in the other and told Graves to make a choice. Graves prudently took his drink with Low and lived to tell the tale.

In late July 1723, Low took a large ship named *Merry Christmas*. He cut extra gun ports in her hull and mounted 34 guns. With this formidable warship and several smaller companions, he took to calling himself "The Pirate Admiral" and sporting a new flag with a red skeleton. He would also hoist a green and yellow flag called "The Green Trumpeter" to summon the captains of his fleet for a meeting.

By August 1723, Low had left the Grand Banks for the South Atlantic, raiding St. Michaels in the Canary Islands and the coast of Africa. He continued his murderous ways, chopping off ears; murdering half of one crew, sparing the other; releasing some ships, burning others. His last recorded capture was a sloop taken near St. Lucia in the eastern Caribbean in May 1724. The sloop's crew reported that Low was down to 30 men. A French warship was said to be on his trail, and finally Low's men seemed to scatter.

Various rumours spread about his demise, but the most common one held that, after a confrontation between Low and his quartermaster, Low shot the man in his sleep. This made the crew rise up against Low. He was abandoned in a boat without provisions, along with two or three of his henchmen. They were picked up by a French vessel from Martinique, recognized, given a quick trial and hanged.

Low had taken an impressive number of vessels, about 140 falling into his hands, 55 of them captured in Atlantic Canada. However, it is his cruelty that stands out. "No one mounted to more lofty attitudes of bloodthirsty unscrupulous wickedness. 'Tis strange that so little has been written or sung of this man," wrote the

Right: A plausible portrait of the grim and scarred face of Ned Low as imagined by a 20th century artist. Below: Treasure hunters claim that the Bay of Fundy's mysterious Isle Haute, seen on the left horizon, holds Ned Low's treasure.

Ned Low torments another victim as Capt. Graves has to make a fateful choice: pistol or punch bowl.

pirate illustrator Howard Pyle in 1921. While other pirates left songs, folklore and treasure legends, Low's legacy was simply a grim catalogue of torture. "What the end was of this repulsive, bloody and uninteresting pirate has never been known," wrote Philip Gosse in *The Pirates' Who's Who* in 1924.

Not until the 1950s, when the American treasure hunter and writer Edward Snow began to claim that Low had buried treasure in Nova Scotia's Bay of Fundy, did any legends, real or invented surface about Low.

However, recent pirate historians, such as Marcus Rediker, see Low as a significant symptom of the escalating war against pirates: "The Golden Age turned crimson." From 1722 onwards, authorities responded to piracy with greater efficiency. As pirates were relentlessly hunted down and exterminated with mass hangings, men like Low responded with extreme and random violence not seen earlier in the Golden Age of Piracy. Whatever the external cause, Low's wild cruelty suggests some deep mental disorder. It is a brutal legacy and a healthy reminder of the grim acts that lurk beneath piracy's romance.

JOHN PHILLIPS AND THE END OF THE GOLDEN AGE

A few hundred Wretches who fear neither God nor Devil, as this Phillips.

Charles Johnson, Pirate Historian, 1724

While Bartholomew Roberts was the most successful pirate to operate in Atlantic Canada, and Ned Low was the most loathsome, the well-documented career of a pirate of lesser rank shows how Canadian waters were central to the Golden Age of Piracy. John Phillips was a pirate who began his career in Newfoundland and finished it at the end of a bloody axe in a watery grave off Nova Scotia. He is one of hundreds of pirates who started their career with one of the more notorious names but branched out to fill the Atlantic with small and short-lived, but destructive, bands of raiders.

Phillips was an English ship's carpenter, a skill much in demand in an era when wooden ships far from home needed constant repairs. On the Grand Banks of Newfoundland in April 1721, his ship was overtaken by the pirate brigantine *Good Fortune*, commanded by Thomas Anstis, a pirate captain who had just broken away from Bartholomew Roberts. Phillips was appointed carpenter of the *Good Fortune*. He had joined a formidable band of pirates, but one with an above-average lust for violence. Their most heinous crime was the vicious gang rape and murder of a female passenger aboard the ship

Thomas Anstis and his men stage a mock pirate trial.

Irwin, an Irish vessel taken off Martinique. A passenger who was beaten trying to stop the rape recalled how, "Twenty one of them forced the poor Creature successively, afterwards broke her Back and flung her into the sea."

After a string of large captures, Anstis' pirates decided to try for a pardon in the summer of 1722, sending a petition to the English King, claiming they had been forced into piracy by Bartholomew Roberts. They passed the time while waiting for a reply on an isolated island off the southwestern tip of Cuba, gambling, dancing, feasting on turtle meat and — most interestingly — holding comic mock-pirate trials where they accused each other of piracy: "Your lordship and gentlemen of the jury, here is a fellow before you that is a sad Dog, a sad, sad Dog and I humbly hope your lordship will order him to be hanged immediately." However after nine months of idle merriment, they learned from a passing ship that their plea for a pardon had been ignored.

Now boasting two large ships they put to sea, but one was wrecked almost immediately and they were soon dogged by a series of Royal Navy ships on their trail. Phillips was ashore on the island of Tobago, converting a newly captured ship into pirate service, when HMS *Winchelsea* arrived. He watched *Good Fortune* disappear over the horizon as Anstis fled, abandoning many of his crew. However Anstis did not have long to live. A few days later his discontented crew killed him as he slept in his hammock and gave up piracy.

Back on Tobago, naval shore parties quickly rounded up most of their shipmates, but Phillips and a handful of the pirates who had managed to elude them ran for their lives and hid in the island jungle. A few weeks later, the trapped men captured a sloop and sailed for England. They burned the sloop in the channel near Bristol in October 1722 and went ashore, splitting up to return to their homes.

After a few months of ease with friends and family in England, Phillips was worried that the law might catch up with him. He had also enjoyed his taste of piracy and wanted more, only this time as captain. Phillips signed aboard a ship heading for Newfoundland, where those who could identify him were few, but those who

The replica brig Niagara, *typical of the navy pirate hunters that brought the Golden Age of Piracy to a close.*

could be recruited were many. He jumped ship in Petty Harbour, just south of St. John's and landed a job splitting cod. Hacking the heads off codfish by day, Phillips quietly sounded out discontented fishermen by night. By August 29, 1723, he had recruited 16 men. His plan was to meet on the beach at darkness and seize one of the many anchored fishing vessels.

His career as pirate captain began almost comically when only four of the 16 recruits showed up. Undaunted, they stole a schooner belonging to William Minott. The pirates named their vessel *Revenge*, chose officers and drew up the rules for "their little Commonwealth." Lacking a Bible, the tiny band swore loyalty to their pirate articles on an axe head. Among their articles were strict rules against desertion, an issue that would bedevil them during their short-lived existence. Phillips was elected captain and everyone else was made an officer except for one lone man who formed the entire crew. The most severe punishment, somewhat unusual in pirate articles, was for rape. Quite possibly Phillips was haunted by that gang rape of the captured passenger off Martinique in his previous pirate company.

The crew soon grew in number. They hoisted a black flag with a death's head and started attacking fishing boats along the coast of Newfoundland. In what would become their standard practice, Phillips' band robbed one ship after another, taking money and provisions while seeking recruits. On September 5, they took three ships in one day. Most of their captures were fishing schooners, but they took one French merchant ship on September 20, 1723, which added a cannon to their arsenal and a cargo of wine to their leisure. They quickly

released most of the captured vessels and crews, but forced skilled men to join them.

One of the pirates recognized a childhood neighbour from Massachusetts, a carpenter aboard the captured fishing sloop *Dolphin*. He was ordered aboard *Revenge* "dead or alive." The reluctant pirate was John Fillmore, the great-grandfather of the thirteenth president of the United States, Millard Fillmore. Another fishing vessel yielded a pirate veteran named John Rose Archer who had sailed with the notorious Blackbeard. The growing band of pirates quickly elected him to the powerful post of quartermaster, in charge of securing and distributing loot. However the move caused some resentment among Phillips' first recruits.

The pirates headed south, capturing ships off Bermuda and Barbados. The captain of one Portuguese brigantine later posted his losses to the pirates, showing how modest the loot often was: £100 in cash, a cask of brandy and three dozen shirts. After that capture, Phillips' luck ran cold. *Revenge* cruised fruitlessly for three months as rations dwindled. At last the crew spotted a large French sloop named *St. Charles* heading to France from Martinique. Boasting ten guns, the sloop easily outgunned Phillips' two cannons and four swivel guns, but the desperate and hungry pirates hoisted their black flag and sailed straight up to the guns declaring that no one would be spared if there was any resistance. The intimidated French

Top Right: A musket ball mould.
Right: Chart of Georges Bank and Cape Sable, the last hunting grounds for Phillips and his men.
Left: Every pirate's nightmare, a heavily armed navy frigate, in this case the Nova Scotia built replica HMS Rose *featured in the film* Master and Commander.

surrendered immediately.

After two more captures, *Revenge* was in need of repairs, so the pirates put in at Tobago to scrape the ship's bottom and replace the main mast. They discovered a sole survivor from Phillips' old ship still there. However, history repeated itself when they also discovered a Royal Navy vessel in the area. Phillips hastily fled the island, leaving four pirates behind.

When the pirates captured another brigantine, three members of the boarding party tried to part company with Phillips. They were led by a carpenter named Fenn, one of Phillips' first four recruits in Newfoundland, who had resented the promotion of John Rose Archer to quartermaster. Fenn, however, did not get far. Firing broke out between the two vessels. One of the runaway pirates was killed, the other was so badly wounded that the carpenter had to amputate his leg with a wood saw. Fenn made another breakaway attempt a week later, and this time Phillips ran him through with a sword and shot him in the head. A day after that, another pirate also tried to leave and Phillips killed him the same way. Fear was soon stalking the pirate's ship, but no one dared act.

On March 25, the pirates captured two ships, both bound for London from Virginia. The young captain of one, named Robert Mortimer, made a courageous bid to recapture his vessel. He struck Phillips with a handspike, one of the heavy wooden bars used to turn the windlass. However Mortimer's own men did not come to his aid. In a rage, Phillips cut Mortimer to pieces. The carpenter from one of the Virginian vessels, Edward Cheeseman, was forced to join the pirates, but immediately began to make plans to take the pirate ship and turn it over to the authorities when the time was ripe.

The pirates now headed north, hunting for ships off Nova Scotia and planning to recruit more pirates in Newfoundland. Lurking off Cape Sable on April 1, they first captured a sloop and then the same day a schooner. Phillips kept the sloop and was planning to scuttle the schooner when he learned that it belonged to Mr. Minott, the owner of his first capture. "We have done him enough injury," he declared in a fit of conscience, ordering the schooner repaired and returned to her captain and crew. That afternoon they spotted another sail, but this vessel did not submit easily. After hours of hard sailing, the pirates finally caught the elusive vessel. The frustrated pirates made the defiant captain, a man with the stout-hearted name of Dependance Ellery, dance about his own deck for hours until he collapsed from exhaustion.

Nova Scotian waters proved rewarding to Phillips and his men. They robbed 11 vessels in quick succession. Their final capture came on April 14, a large, brand-new Massachusetts' sloop named *Squirrel*, belonging to Andrew

Haraden. The pirates liked the look of this vessel and took it over, releasing the captured crew — except for Captain Haraden — in the worn-out *Revenge*. Cheeseman, the reluctant pirate carpenter who was quietly plotting Phillips' downfall, took Haraden into his confidence and three days later they mounted their takeover attempt.

Cheeseman had noted Phillips' ruthless execution of dissenting crewmen, so he planned his attack with merciless precision. He used some morning repairs as an excuse to leave his tools on deck. Phillips was below plotting a course. The pirate sailing master, a massive man named Nutt, was in command, backed up by the pirate boatswain, while Archer the quartermaster was pouring lead musket balls in the hold.

At noon, Cheeseman fetched a bottle of brandy and poured out a drink for all on deck, toasting the pirate officers. "To Their next Merry Meeting!" he declared, as one of his confederates quietly picked up a carpenter's axe, looked at Cheeseman and winked — the signal to begin. Cheeseman grabbed the unsuspecting Nutt by his collar and hurled him over the side. At the same time, the axe crashed into the boatswain's skull, neatly splitting it in two. However, as Nutt went over the side, he grabbed Cheeseman's sleeve and cried, "Lord have mercy upon me! What are you going to do, carpenter?" "Master you are a dead man," Cheeseman replied and calmly broke the man's grasp, sending him into the deep.

The noise brought Phillips racing to the deck, where Cheeseman "saluted" him with a mallet, breaking his jaw. The pirate gunner rushed to Phillips' defence, but was tripped by Cheeseman and thrown into the sea. Still standing, John Phillips, who had escaped so many battles, shipwrecks and marooning was quickly finished off by a carpenter's axe.

Cheeseman leapt into the hold to strangle the last pirate officer, the quartermaster and old Blackbeard veteran, John Rose Archer, but one young sailor reminded him that they needed a pirate officer as witness to prove that they were forced men. The body of the dead pirate captain was thrown overboard, but Cheeseman, remembering the capture of Blackbeard a few years earlier, added a gruesome touch. He hacked off Phillips' head and pickled it in salt. As Haraden resumed command of his sloop and sailed into Boston, the head was mounted on the sloop's masthead.

The surviving pirates were tried in Boston. Most were able to prove they were forced into piracy or had assisted in the mutiny and were acquitted. The rest went to the gallows on June 2, 1724. Urged on by Cotton Mather, the Puritan minister famous for his zealous moralizing, they made much-publicized pious confessions. Archer blamed drink, but added a telling protest on the gallows making a plea: "I would wish that Masters of Vessels would not use their men with so much severity, as many of them do, which exposes us to great temptations." To make brutally clear the cost of such temptations, the court had Archer's body gibbeted. It was coated in tar and hung in chains

on Bird Island in Boston Harbor. Above the rotting skeleton flew John Phillips' ragged black flag. In Phillips' nine-month career as a pirate captain, 34 ships had fallen to his flag, about 15 of them in Canadian waters.

By the time Phillips' men met their end, piracy in the Atlantic Ocean was in retreat. The killing of Edward Teach (Blackbeard) in 1718 and of Bartholomew Roberts in 1722 were turning points. While governments had at first tried to pardon pirates or enlist them as privateers, neither approach had worked. Instead, the number of British naval ships in the colonies was tripled to suppress piracy. In Newfoundland, the Navy's two small station ships were replaced with three larger warships. The French Navy, which had never assigned ships to the fishery, now sent two warships to Newfoundland. They captured one pirate ship and sank another in 1724.

New, determined and merciless colonial governors were sent out to try and execute pirates. Draconian anti-piracy laws were put at their disposal, administered by a new system of powerful Admiralty Courts set up throughout the British Empire. The mass hangings that followed killed pirates by the hundreds. Piracy itself did not disappear. In fact, it returned to flourish in other parts of the world. However, the deep pool of pirates, their bold leaders, unique rebel culture and even the black pirate flags themselves disappeared from the waters of Atlantic Canada.

PIRATES, MUTINEERS AND WRECKERS IN THE AGE OF SAIL

John, we are in the hands of enemies.
We must either die or live and must do something to save our lives.

William Carr, reluctant pirate, *Saladin*, 1844

After the Golden Age of Piracy was crushed in the 1720s, piracy in the Atlantic went into decline — but it never completely disappeared. The last serious pirates based in the region were the merciless husband-and-wife team of Eric and Maria Cobham. They settled on the isolated west coast of Newfoundland at Sandy Point in 1740 and preyed on the growing fur trade from the Saint Lawrence. Their strategy, to avoid the now serious enforcement of piracy laws, was to leave no survivors.

Pirates in the Golden Age usually killed selectively, murdering and torturing select victims, but releasing the rest. The Cobhams, however, killed everyone they captured and scuttled their ships to camouflage the murders as shipwrecks. Maria Cobham dressed in the uniform of a dead British naval officer and savoured cruel ways of killing. She once tied the captain and two mates of a captured ship to a capstan and used them for target practice. Around 1760 the Cobhams retired to France, where Maria slowly poisoned herself to death with opium. Eric wrote a boastful, confessional autobiography on his deathbed in 1780.

The authorities in the struggling colonies of Atlantic Canada in the eighteenth century were too weak to capture and try pirates, but by the nineteenth century the region was maturing.

Pirates in disguise attempt to lure a 19th century merchant ship.

Nova Scotia, New Brunswick and Prince Edward Island had growing populations and soon emerged as major shipbuilding centres. Newfoundland's seasonal fishing settlements grew into permanent communities. These colonies now had fully functioning courts that inherited the draconian anti-piracy laws of the eighteenth century. Piracy was so serious that the penalty was not only death, but also ritualistic execution.

A powerful, special Admiralty Court tried and executed pirates. They were hanged in the mud on the beach, between high and low tide, to express the jurisdiction of the Admiralty Court over the sea. The bodies were often left hanging for the sea to wash over for several tides. Then the corpse would be tarred and hanged in chains in a gibbet at the harbour entrance as a warning to other mariners. Most of those convicted of piracy in Atlantic Canada after the 1700s never accomplished more than the theft of a single ship or the occasional shipboard murder. Nevertheless, the courts required that their corpses decorate prominent parts of the harbour as a warning to other sailors. In St. John's the Narrows was used as a gibbet site. In Halifax, gibbets were erected at different times at Georges Island, McNabs Island and Point Pleasant.

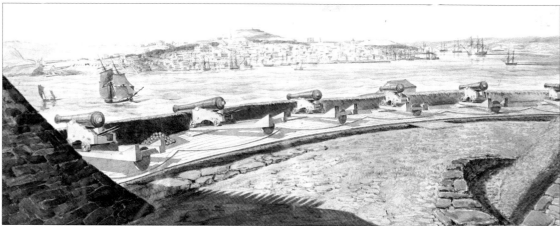

Top: A rare view from 1782 showing the point at Black Rock Beach in Halifax where Edward Jordan's body was gibbeted.

🌀 Above: The bustling Halifax waterfront in 1801, the scene of Jordan's pirate trial.

Such executions could make for a macabre spectacle, as in 1809 when Halifax offered a weird welcome to all arriving ships — gibbets on either side of the harbour. A bloody naval mutiny aboard HMS *Columbine* resulted in four rotting corpses swinging in the wind on the aptly named Hangman's Beach on McNabs Island. On the other side of the harbour, a lone corpse dangled at Black Rock Beach at Point Pleasant, the body of pirate Edward Jordan. He was a former Irish rebel who had settled in the Gaspé Bay area as a fisherman trading with Halifax merchants. His schooner, the *Three Sisters*, named after his daughters, was seized for debts he owed to a Halifax merchant. Off Canso, Jordan and his wife Margaret attacked the crew manning the merchant's vessel. They killed two sailors and wounded the captain, John Stairs, who jumped overboard to escape.

🏴 *Top: Black Rock Beach at Point Pleasant Park with McNabs Island in the distance, favoured locations for gibbets (digitally added).*
Bottom: The grim pirate relic of Edward Jordan's skull, preserved for generations at the Nova Scotia Museum.

Miraculously, Stairs was rescued a few hours later by an American fishing schooner. Jordan fled with his family to Newfoundland, where he tried to recruit a crew to sail the *Three Sisters* to Ireland. However, on the Grand Banks, the Navy schooner HMS *Cuttle* caught up with him. He submitted meekly, crying out, "The Lord have mercy on me, what will my poor children do?"

Jordan was tried for piracy in Halifax, and on November 23, 1809, he was hanged at Freshwater Beach, where Pier 21 stands today. After the execution, his body was taken down, tarred and hanged in chains in a gibbet mounted on the ruins of an old gun battery at Black Rock Beach in Point Pleasant Park. His wife Margaret was not charged as she had played a relatively minor part in the killings and many felt sorry for her. Halifax residents raised money to return the destitute Margaret and her three daughters to Ireland.

Jordan's body stood in rusty decay for many years, as it was a serious offence to tamper with a gibbet. According to legend it was the horror-struck daughter of the Lieutenant-Governor who had it taken down when she unexpectedly discovered it while riding in Point Pleasant Park. His remaining bones were given a shallow burial in the ruins of the old battery. In 1844, when a fresh piracy trial reawakened interest in pirate lore, a

Top: The entrance to Halifax Harbour where hanging pirate bodies welcomed mariners.

💲*Left: Replica at the Maritime Museum of the Atlantic of pirate Jordan's gibbet.*

Mr. Williamson dug up Jordan's skull, still circled by the iron ring from the gibbet. He gave the skull to the Mechanic's Institute, the forerunner of the Nova Scotia Museum. The skull became a curio at the museum for generations, although the iron ring disappeared in the late nineteenth century. The cranium of the skull survives today, bearing several generations of inscriptions by Museum staff. It serves as a reminder of the bizarre public execution rituals of the Age of Piracy.

During Atlantic Canada's rise as a major shipping power in the 1800s, piracy was feared but rarely encountered. Fishermen on Newfoundland's Grand Banks still lived with the dangers of weather and work, but pirate attacks became a distant memory. Vessels from the growing merchant fleets of New Brunswick and Nova

Scotia could safely trade all over the world, protected by the flag of the British Empire and its powerful navy. However, certain areas of the Caribbean, the North African Coast and the South China Sea still saw the occasional pirate attack.

Piracy became so rare after 1815 that most civilian ships stopped carrying cannons to defend themselves. Only false gun ports remained painted on hulls where once real gun ports and cannons had been mounted. Some historians today feel this was a ruse to suggest that a ship mounted many cannons, as a deterrence against pirate attack. Others feel the practice had more to do with aesthetics than defence. It did remain most popular in ships that traded in the Pacific and Mediterranean, where pirates still lingered.

In fact, in the nineteenth century it was China where piracy blossomed. Taking advantage of a Chinese government weakened by European incursions, Chinese piracy exploded in the South China Sea in the early 1800s. Its most noted leader was Zheng Yi, who formed a coalition of pirates that was estimated to reach 10,000 men by 1804. After his death in 1807 his wife, Zheng Yi Sao, also known as Ching Shih, took over. Her captures exceeded even Bartholomew Roberts' success until famine, naval attacks and dissension broke up her forces in the 1820s. Ships from Nova Scotia and New Brunswick sailing these waters did so nervously. However, Britain, using diplomacy when necessary and military attacks when convenient, crushed pirate settlements whenever they presented a serious threat to British shipping.

Another area where pockets of piracy remained was the Caribbean. On April 28, 1840, the brig *Vernon* from Shelburne, Nova Scotia, was headed to Halifax with a cargo of Jamaican rum. Just past Cape San Antonio at the far west end of Cuba, seven heavily armed men swarmed aboard from a small boat. Led by a pirate named Francisco Denis, they forced *Vernon's* crew to unload the rum on an isolated island near the cape. As the Nova Scotians rolled the barrels into the pirate's lair, they grimly noted the shattered name board of *Swallow*, a schooner from Liverpool, Nova Scotia, which had disappeared a few years before — clearly a victim of the same pirates.

The pirates killed *Vernon's* captain and two of his crew before burning the looted brig. One Nova Scotian named Ben Peach jumped overboard and escaped. He was found injured and naked a day later by a Spanish schooner. The schooner's owner, Antonio Peloso, set a cunning trap for the pirates. He boldly rowed ashore alone and offered to join the pirates, inviting them to first dine aboard his schooner. At a prearranged signal, Peloso's crew attacked the pirates, disarmed them and then went ashore to rescue the rest of *Vernon's* crew. The pirates and *Vernon's* survivors were taken to Havana.

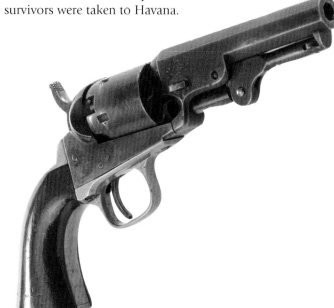

🜚 *Opposite: The brig* Florence *in 1857, a close match to the brig* Vernon.
Right: Colt naval revolver, often carried by merchant captains.

Horrible Massacre

OF THE

COMMANDER AND OFFICERS OF THE SALADIN,

And subsequent Murder of the Chief Mutineer.

...donia steamer, from Boston and Halifax, arrived at Liverpool on Saturday, fully confirms the account of piracy on board the Saladin, and massacre of her commander and officers, some few particulars of which appeared in the 'Advertiser' of last week. The subjoined account was received at Lloyd's on Saturday afternoon, and unfolds the deep mystery attached to this, one of the most heart-rending cases of wholesale murder which of late years has been brought to our notice.

"George Jones first joined Saladin at Valparaiso, crew twelve in number, and two others (Capt. Fielding and son George)—was working my passage as sail-maker, but acted as steward, by Captain M'Kenzie's request, until after passing Cape Horn, when John Galloway took the situation, and I repaired some of the sails. While in the cabin as steward frequent differences arose between Capt. M'Kenzie and Capt Fielding. The latter used to come to me and tell me what he had said, and about his quarrels with Captain M'Kenzie; then talk of the amount of money on board, and what a fine prize a pirate would make of them; asked me if I would fight against them, if attacked—he would not. Captain M Kenzie used to drink a great deal. Fielding, on one occasion, said to me, 'Now, Jones, if you want to save your life, now is the time. I have spoken to the carpenter, and I intend to be master of this vessel.' At another time Fielding, in my presence, made a motion to show he would cut Captain M'Kenzie's throat, saying, at the same time, 'Damn you." When I attempted to acquaint Captain M'Kenzie of it, he threatened my life. I...

an axe. I think Anderson also struck him. Fielding, Johnson, and Anderson threw the body overboard. Nothing more was done for a quarter of an hour, when the Captain rung his bell three or four times, but no answer was given to it. Fielding and the others went to the main deck, and I heard nothing for some time, until I heard the carpenter's voice in the water This alarmed me, as I understood the Captain was to be killed before the carpenter was to be disturbed, and I exclaimed, 'Oh, Lord, there is a man overboard.' With this Fielding ran immediately on the poop, and shouted a man overboard as loud as he could, the Swede following him. Capt. M'Kenzie ran out of the companion, and as he came up Anderson struck him; the blow did not kill him, he ran after Anderson round the companion. Fielding then called to me, 'D—n you, why don't you run after him? If you don't lay hold of him, I will give you a clout that will kill you.' I left go the helm, and went round the companion, and the Swede and Captain M'Kenzie were struggleing together. Fielding again said, 'D—n you, why don't you lay hold of him?' I then took hold of his hands, and Fielding struck him two blows with the axe which killed him. Fielding hauled him forward in front of the companion, and struck him again; the Swede and Fielding threw him overboard. When the man come to relieve the helm, they agreed to take his life, during this time Collins came on deck, and went he the head; when the watch was called Jem came up, he went to the helm, Anderson struck him, as I understood, with a hammer, and he was thrown overboard. I heard no noise in the boat. The other two men, Moffatt and Collins, who had gone down again, were then called up. They came, and Moffat sat down on the spar, forepar of the galley, Hazleton struck him, as I understood with an axe, and killed him. I heard the blow, and after I came out of the boat I saw his body. I assisted Anderson and Johnston in throwing the body overboard. Before Moffat was thrown overboard Anderson went forward, struck Collins on the head, and he fell into the water. I did not see the blow, but I heard Collin's exclamation on receiving it. Some time after this it was proposed by Fielding to do away with the cook, Carr, and the steward, Galloway, but the rest would not consent. Filding said he would let them work, but he would find a way get rid of them. The cook came aft about six o'clock; was alarmed when Captain Fielding told him the ship was ours, that all the crew remaining were on the poop. The cook asked what it meant; he

Above, left to right: The Saladin *pirates — William Carr, William Trevaskiss, Charles Anderson, George Jones, John Hazelton and John Galloway.*
Below: A boarding pike from the home of a privateersman in Liverpool, Nova Scotia.

Suspected of many previous attacks, the pirates were convicted and on July 22, 1840, they were shot and then beheaded on the Havana waterfront. The head of pirate Captain Denis was mounted on a pole at Cape San Antonio, while the heads of his men decorated the entrance to Havana Harbour.

Frightening as such attacks were, they became more and more of a rarity. However, as pirate attacks nearly disappeared, they were eclipsed by a more serious threat to the ships of Atlantic Canada, a threat that came from within. The delicate balance of authority on an isolated sailing ship sometimes exploded into mutiny when aggrieved or greedy sailors took over the vessel. By law, these mutinies constituted piracy, but judges and juries usually preferred the lesser charge of murder because the gruesome display of bodies in gibbets offended Victorian values.

The biggest piracy trial in the region occurred in 1844 when "a fiend in human form" named George Fielding led a mutiny aboard the British barque *Saladin*. When *Saladin* left Valparaiso, Chile, for Liverpool, England, Fielding — a smuggler who had escaped from a Peruvian prison — was a passenger. He discovered that *Saladin* was carrying almost 8,000 silver dollars and 13 bars of silver, in addition to its cargo of copper and fertilizer. Using fear and greed, Fielding manipu-

lated one half of *Saladin's* crew to kill the other half for the treasure. Just after *Saladin* crossed the equator at midnight on April 14, 1844, the captain, officers and many of the crew were butchered and thrown overboard. A day later, the mutineers turned on Fielding, killing him and his 12-year-old son. They hoped to hide the treasure on an island, sink the ship and escape in a small boat, but *Saladin* sailed off course and ran aground at Country Harbour on Nova Scotia's Eastern Shore.

The captain of a coastal schooner, William Cunningham, stopped to assist the stranded ship, but was startled by what he found on board: piles of treasure, burned letters, missing officers and a very drunk group of sailors. Among the litter of paper was a London literary magazine torn open to a short story entitled "The Successful Mutiny." He secretly alerted the authorities while he helped *Saladin's* crew secure the ship. A few days later the six men were arrested and taken to Halifax.

They faced the last piracy trial held in Nova Scotia. After some legal wrangling the courts decided that piracy, which would require the convicted to be gibbeted, was too unseemly for Victorian sensibilities. The six men were indicted on the lesser charge of murder. Two convinced the court that they had been forced to join the

pirates and were acquitted. The other four were hanged on July 30, 1844. One of the survivors, William Carr, settled down near Digby to lead an honest and sober life, except it is said, every year on the April 14 anniversary of the murders, he would get roaring drunk.

The wreck of *Saladin* was soon torn to pieces by the sea, but most of her contents were salvaged. The treasure was returned to its owners. The rest was sold at auction. Many curios of *Saladin* were retained by families around Nova Scotia, most notably the mysterious ship's figurehead. Historians debate whether it is really from *Saladin*, but it has always looked the part.

The *Saladin* mutineers may not fit the mythic definition of pirates, but they were pirates in the eyes of the law and were typical of those many pirates who often began their careers with mutiny. They also referred to themselves as pirates, swore piratical oaths and even talked of burying treasure.

One of the last fatal acts of piratical ship attack in the Atlantic region was pulled off by a band of Civil War desperados in 1863. A Confederate schemer, the aptly named John C. Brain, recruited a number of would-be pirates in Saint John, New Brunswick,

❧ Left: A figurehead, reputed by legend to be from the cursed *Saladin*.
❧ Opposite: The mutineers used the ship's Bible, preserved at the Maritime Museum of the Atlantic, to swear piratical oaths.

in 1863. They captured the Portland to New York steamer *Chesapeake*, killing one of the ship's engineers. They carried a forged Letter of Marque, but were by any definition of the law pirates.

The Union Navy caught the pirates in Nova Scotian waters near Halifax and brought them and their captured ship into the city. Diplomatic and judicial disputes broke out as the Confederates claimed the ship as a capture of war and the Union Government pushed for the crew to be hanged as pirates. In the end, the ship was returned to its owners, but the pirates themselves managed to escape thanks to a jailbreak engineered by some wealthy Haligonians who were sympathetic to the Confederacy.

A mutiny near Liverpool, Nova Scotia, in 1865 led to a controversial but less well-known trial. John Douglas was the mate of the brigantine *Zero* and led the mutiny that resulted in the murder of *Zero's* captain. The mutineers tried to sink the ship to hide the evidence, but failed and were soon caught. At the trial, Douglas managed to pin the murder on the brigantine's cook, an African Nova Scotian named Henry Dowsey. Douglas escaped with a life sentence, but Dowsey was sentenced to death. This touched off a province-wide protest, as many felt that Dowsey was unjustly selected for blame as he was the only African sailor on board. In most mutinies, the ringleader is considered equally guilty, regardless of who does any killing. However, the protests were in vain and Dowsey went to the hangman.

The Yarmouth ship *Lennie* was seized in a mutiny in the English Channel in 1875. Led by a murderous sailor known as "Big Harry," mutineers killed all the ship's officers and planned to murder the rest of the crew, sail to Greece and sell off her cargo. However, a courageous steward, Constant Van Hoydonck, prevented further killings, tricked the mutineers into running aground on the French coast and alerted the police with a message in a bottle. The mutineers were captured and hanged. Van Hoydonck received a large reward and left the sea to open a pub in London.

One of the last acts of bloody mayhem dealt with in Nova Scotia took place on the American barquentine *Herbert Fuller*. On July 21, 1896, the vessel came to anchor in Halifax Harbour with a bloody secret. She carried the bodies of her captain, his wife and the second mate, who were hacked to death by an unknown member of her crew while the vessel was off the coast of Nova Scotia. The baffled and frightened surviving crew put into Halifax and called the police aboard.

The *Herbert Fuller* murders became a celebrated "whodunit" mystery. The first mate, Tom Bram, was convicted in New York of the murders later that year. However, he was pardoned in 1919 by President Woodrow Wilson, who felt that the African American sailor had not received a fair trial. The mystery was never satisfactorily solved. All that remains today are the ghastly pictures of blood-splattered and wrecked cabins aboard *Herbert Fuller*, photographs that were taken aboard the barquentine in 1896 by Halifax police officers to gather evidence for the American authorities. The new medium of photography had captured the very old tradition of blood-soaked decks, a chilling reminder of the consequences of violence that lurk behind piracy's romantic myth.

There was one other lingering vestige of piracy in Atlantic Canada that survived at least until the early nineteenth century: a subspecies of pirates known as "wreckers." These were thieves who camped out on remote capes and islands where ships could come to grief. They sometimes lit false fires to lure vessels into danger and would murder any survivors to cover up their ill-gotten salvage of surviving valuables.

Above: Barquentine Herbert Fuller *anchored in Halifax in 1896 as the police search for evidence.*
🖲 *Right, from top to bottom: The bloodstained* Herbert Fuller *crime scene photographs: main cabin passageway; 2nd Mate's cabin; Mrs. Nash's cabin.*

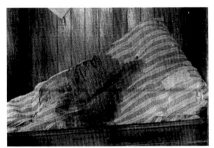

The term "wreckers" was also used to describe salvagers, people who played no role in causing a shipwreck and, in fact, who often helped rescue survivors, but who then enthusiastically helped themselves to the wreckage without bothering with the legal niceties of salvage laws. Many communities in Atlantic Canada benefited from illegal salvage, and, in fact, the practice often provided vital income for isolated coastal communities. However, despite the often generous acts of humanity shown by such communities in rescuing and caring for survivors, suspicions were endlessly raised about their culpability.

One of the rare documented examples of wrecking took place in the Bay of Fundy in a Nova Scotian community now known as Margaretsville. On December 30, 1796, the robbed and mutilated bodies of Patrick McMaster and William Harris were found on the beach beside the wreck of their small schooner. Four more victims were later found and suspicions fell on the only settler in the area, a man named Peter Barnes. Nothing was ever proved, but rumours lingered for years that, desperate for supplies, he lit a false fire, luring the schooner to its doom. For a time the community was known as Peter's Point. Barnes remained ostracized as the community of Margretsville grew up around him. According to Margaretsville legend, Barnes eventually died one night 20 years after the wreck when, in a twist of poetic justice, he lost his way in a blinding winter storm and fell over the cliff to die on the very beach of his crime.

Many isolated stretches of the Newfoundland coast, including Bartholomew Roberts' old haunt at Trepassey, were rumoured to harbour wreckers, as well as remote stretches of the Gulf of Saint Lawrence, parts of Cape Breton and the Seal Island area of southwest Nova Scotia. Sable Island was believed to be the most popular location for wreckers. There were regular camps of men at Sable who hunted seals and salvaged the island's many shipwrecks. Rumours circulated that they murdered survivors and mutilated bodies. These suspicions built support for Nova Scotia's Governor to establish a rescue station on the island in 1801, led by Superintendent James Morris. He soon evicted the last of the wreckers, although there was never any proof that they had lured ships or murdered their crews.

PIRATE LIFE

*In an honest service, there is thin commons — low wages, and hard labour. In this,
plenty ... pleasure and ease, liberty and power! Who would not balance on this side,
when all the hazard that is run for it, at worst is only a sour look or two at choking?
No, a merry life and a short one shall be my motto!*

Bartholomew Roberts, 1720

Throughout history, pirates were thieves and murderers whose lives were mostly cruel and short. However, in certain times and places, they created their own outlaw culture, carving out societies of wild rebel freedom that turned the rules of their age upside down. The Golden Age of Piracy from 1690 to 1730 was one such time. Pirates were so numerous in this era that they created a short-lived but deeply subversive way of life with remarkable levels of democracy and its own strict codes of behaviour. Its allure was so powerful that we can still see distorted versions of it in popular culture today.

Pirate life in this golden period was defined by "The Articles," a list of rules for life aboard that formed a kind of constitution. All kinds of ships — merchant, fishing and naval — used articles. Merchant and fishing articles listed wages and rations and contract restrictions. Naval articles were a long and grim list of absolute duties and brutal punishments known as the Articles of War. Pirate articles drew from earlier buccaneering customs. They were short, practical and, for their times, notably egalitarian. A pirate recruit signed and swore an oath on a Bible (or often an axe or cannon) to obey the

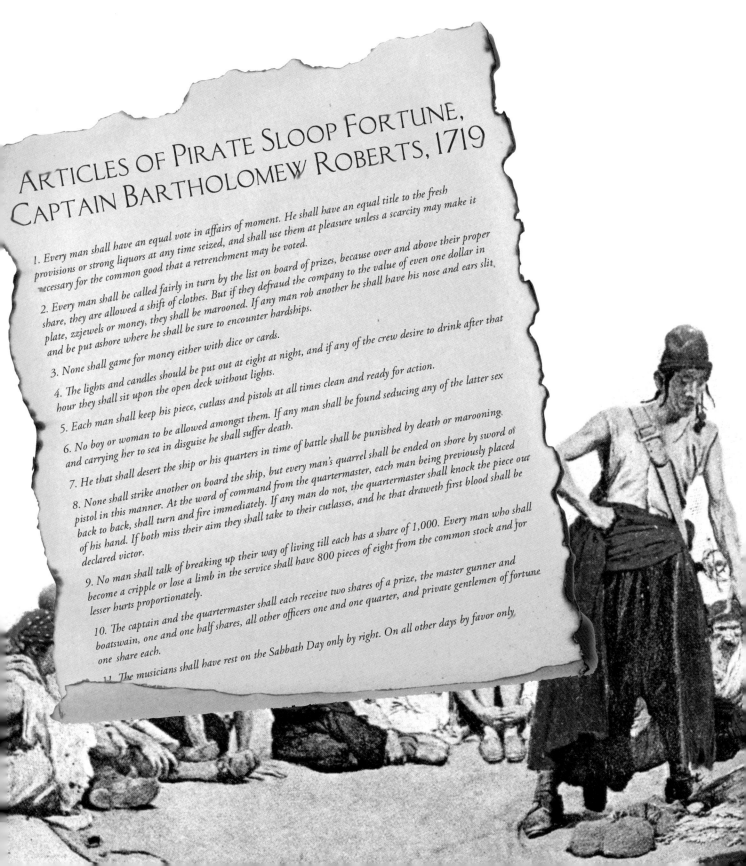

ARTICLES OF PIRATE SLOOP FORTUNE, CAPTAIN BARTHOLOMEW ROBERTS, 1719

1. Every man shall have an equal vote in affairs of moment. He shall have an equal title to the fresh provisions or strong liquors at any time seized, and shall use them at pleasure unless a scarcity may make it necessary for the common good that a retrenchment may be voted.

2. Every man shall be called fairly in turn by the list on board of prizes, because over and above their proper share, they are allowed a shift of clothes. But if they defraud the company to the value of even one dollar in plate, zzjewels or money, they shall be marooned. If any man rob another he shall have his nose and ears slit, and be put ashore where he shall be sure to encounter hardships.

3. None shall game for money either with dice or cards.

4. The lights and candles should be put out at eight at night, and if any of the crew desire to drink after that hour they shall sit upon the open deck without lights.

5. Each man shall keep his piece, cutlass and pistols at all times clean and ready for action.

6. No boy or woman to be allowed amongst them. If any man shall be found seducing any of the latter sex and carrying her to sea in disguise he shall suffer death.

7. He that shall desert the ship or his quarters in time of battle shall be punished by death or marooning.

8. None shall strike another on board the ship, but every man's quarrel shall be ended on shore by sword or pistol in this manner. At the word of command from the quartermaster, each man being previously placed back to back, shall turn and fire immediately. If any man do not, the quartermaster shall knock the piece out of his hand. If both miss their aim they shall take to their cutlasses, and he that draweth first blood shall be declared victor.

9. No man shall talk of breaking up their way of living till each has a share of 1,000. Every man who shall become a cripple or lose a limb in the service shall have 800 pieces of eight from the common stock and for lesser hurts proportionately.

10. The captain and the quartermaster shall each receive two shares of a prize, the master gunner and boatswain, one and one half shares, all other officers one and one quarter, and private gentlemen of fortune one share each.

11. The musicians shall have rest on the Sabbath Day only by right. On all other days by favor only.

articles. Once you signed the articles, you became a pirate. When pirates were captured, the articles became a key piece of evidence to convict them. Pirate articles for Bartholomew Roberts, Ned Low and John Phillips have survived, giving us a detailed glimpse at a life that was harsh but remarkably free and equal.

Pirate articles drew on common custom, but varied considerably according to the priorities and nature of individual crews. Central to all was the issue of sharing the loot. All war ships — whether naval, privateer or pirate — divided their plunder into shares to pay their crews. Pirates were unique because they shared almost equally. A naval captain would typically receive a share about 150 times more than that of an ordinary sailor. A privateer captain would receive 10 times more. However, a pirate captain received only double the share of the rank-and-file pirate. Joining a pirate crew was often called "going on the account," as it marked a move from wages to collective ownership.

Standard in almost every set of pirate articles was a disability clause, an early pension plan that awarded generous amounts to those who were injured, usually starting at 600 to 800 pieces of eight for a limb. It was a bold collective measure at a time when pensions and injury awards were unheard of in merchant and

Pirates dividing their loot as depicted by Howard Pyle. Pirates did not bury treasure, but took the division of loot very seriously.

fishing vessels and only being put forward in rudimentary fashion in Britain's Royal Navy.

Many pirate articles spell out rough-and-ready ways of settling disputes, banning duels on board ship, but setting out rules for their conduct on land. One pirate legend that is solidly founded in fact is the practice of marooning. For serious offences, such as desertion in battle or theft from the common loot, the miscreant would be abandoned on a desolate island where he would be sure to encounter hardship. Sometimes the articles would spell out that he would be supplied "with one Bottle of Powder, one Bottle of Water, one small Arm, and Shot."

So associated with piracy was this punishment that pirates often called themselves "Marooners." At other times, in a patriotic mood, they would call themselves privateers, but the term they most often used to describe themselves was "Gentlemen of Fortune," a proud reflection that they lived by what they captured and that they answered to no master but chance.

Drinking and carousing was another very real facet of pirate life. There are numerous accounts of almost unlimited merry and rowdy drinking by pirate crews. However, pirates also took measures to regulate their most popular pastime with punishments for drunkenness and even "lights-out" rules. Many pirate ships also banned gambling, as a way of avoiding the often fatal disputes that resulted from it.

❈   ❈   ❈

Numerous accounts from piracy's Golden Age indicate that captains of pirate ships were chosen collectively by the crew. Bartholomew Roberts' career began when he was elected, and his followers made it clear that they "permitted him to hold this office only on condition that they might as a body

be master over him." Most pirate crews also selected a quartermaster, who could balance the authority of the captain and, most significantly, take responsibility for securing and dividing the loot.

Contrary to the popular impression that pirate captains were tyrants, the authority of pirate captains was limited to decisions of navigation and battle. Ned Low's surgeon was able to punch his injured captain with impunity because the captain's limited authority was overruled by the great value the crew placed in having a surgeon aboard. When Low attacked his crew's quartermaster, he was quickly deposed.

Pirates often enacted their own version of justice. Wholesale murder of captives was rare. Their violence was selective, directed at crews who resisted, groups they disliked and authority figures. It was most often the captain of a captured ship who faced possible death or torture. John Phillips beat and abused a merchant named John Wingfield whom he had captured, berating him as a "Son of a Bitch that starved the men and that it was such Dogs as he that put men on Pyrating." In fact some pirates conducted impromptu shipboard trials. Captured sailors where questioned about their former captains. Was he honest and humane or cruel and corrupt? The captain's fate hung on their answers.

However, equality and democracy aboard pirate ships only went so far. While some pirates welcomed escaped slaves as equals, others saw them as merely human cargo to be abandoned or sold. Some pirates, like Ned Low, directed jingoistic hatred towards certain nationalities, be it the French, Spanish or New Englanders. And all pirates drew a distinction between volunteers, who drew the full benefit of their rebel society, and forced men, whose status was precarious

until they signed the articles and took the full risk of being a pirate.

⊠   ⊠   ⊠

The pirates of the early eighteenth century created one of the world's great visual symbols: the skull and crossbones flag, known as the Jolly Roger. No one is certain where the term comes from. This flag is now associated with pirates from all periods, but it was actually only used during the first two decades of the 1700s. Pirates from the buccaneering period usually flew a red flag. In 1700, the first reports begin of black flags, adorned with skulls and a skeleton. It was a never-forgotten weapon of terror. The goal was to frighten merchant ships into surrendering without a fight.

Pirates customized their flags, creating a wide variety of Jolly Rogers that went far beyond the familiar skull and crossbones. Individual captains and crews drew from the rich language of death symbols often seen on eighteenth-century grave markers. The most common element was the skull or "death's head." It was often adorned with bones. On a grave marker the skull means "Repent Before you Die." On a pirate flag it means "Surrender or Die."

Other pirates used full skeletons or white corpses called "anatomies." Hourglasses were often depicted, meaning "your time is running out." Hearts represented not love but life and death. Swords and pikes rounded out the menacing iconography.

There are numerous period reports of the use of these "Black Flags" and "Death Flags" aboard pirate ships. The making and hoisting of their own flag was one of the key events in forming a

new pirate crew. Colonial governors would often complete the cycle by hoisting the Jolly Roger as they hanged pirates.

Although pirates ceased using the Jolly Roger after the 1720s, its powerful image became a ready-made symbol for outlaws in the twentieth century. In World War I, British Admiral Arthur Knyvet Wilson declared that the crews of all submarines should be hanged as pirates, and as a result many British submariners defiantly adopted the skull and crossbones. They were followed by countless other rebels and would-be rebels, from motorcycle gangs to computer software pirates.

⊠ ⊠ ⊠

Pirates have always adapted and subverted the weapons of their age. Unlike naval ships, pirate vessels seldom depended on mass firepower from large cannons, but on lethal short-range weapons with which they could cripple and board their prey. Only a few of the major pirates, such as Easton, Roberts or Teach, showed a flare for gunnery to disable a ship at a distance. Long-range gunnery required much hard work and regular drills. Most pirates valued cannons mainly as close-range anti-personnel weapons and for their intimidation value. Swivel guns — small pivoting cannons — were very popular as they could be quickly loaded and aimed and were often taken up into the rigging. Pirate cannons came from a bewildering range of sources and were taken from one ship to another.

Top: An early French "Jolly Roger" pirate flag.
Middle: A variation often attributed to pirate Jack Rackham.
Bottom: The grave marker imagery which inspired pirate flags.

Many were old and outlived the sailors who fired them.

Small arms, pistols and muskets were the pirates' main weapons. Ned Low's pirate articles promised, "He that sees a Sail first, shall have the best Pistol or Small Arm aboard of her." Pirates jealously treasured their personal weapons and pirate articles had strict instructions that every pirate had to keep his own weapons clean and ready for service or face severe penalties. However, flintlock pistols were essentially good for only one shot in a close fight, after which many were designed to be used as clubs. Eyewitnesses describe how pirate pistols were often decorated with colourful silk ribbons that also acted as lanyards to tie the pistols to belts

Above: An 18th century hand grenade, often used in ship-to-ship battles.
Right: Pirate battles often became ruthless close-range fights as pistol fire gave way to bludgeoning.

Left: The blunderbuss, an indispensable boarding weapon, devastating at short range.

so they would not be dropped and lost overboard.

Pirates also employed the many edged weapons of the age, most commonly the ubiquitous cutlass, a broad, heavy hacking sword. However, a wide variety of knives, daggers, pikes and axes were also essential. Pirates were also adept with "infernal weapons," such as grenades and stink bombs, which could play a key role in crippling and disorganizing any resistance.

⊗　　⊗　　⊗

When we imagine what pirates look like, we imagine early eighteenth-century clothes, because that period is the Golden Age of Piracy in the Atlantic Ocean. Tricorn hats, buckled shoes, breeches and stockings were all standard clothes for eighteenth-century sailors. Generations of romantic writers in book and film have made their fictional pirates more ornate and aristocratic. However, large-plumed hats and richly embroidered coats were only worn by the occasional captain such as Bartholomew Roberts. Most accounts of pirates indicate that they wore rough and simple clothes, most often in rags. Pirates who boarded captured ships were rewarded with first pick of the best clothes. For brief periods some pirates could accumulate some splendour. Ned Low's men in 1722 are described as each having "several Pieces of Linnen Cloth, Pieces of Silk, spare hats, Shoes, Stockings, and Gold Lace." However

their fine clothes were quickly traded, worn out or given away.

Somewhat surprisingly, pirates in the Golden Age did not wear tattoos or earrings. Tattoos did not become popular with sailors until the 1780s, after James Cook's and other ships sailed to the Pacific, where sailors quickly embraced the rich tradition of Polynesian tattoos. Earrings had been fashionable with the buccaneers of the 1600s, but not a single account of pirates in the 1700s mentions them — except as loot stored in a sea chest!

⊗　　⊗　　⊗

Female pirates were very rare and, in fact, surviving ships' articles of pirate ships make it clear that they were forbidden to join. However, the Golden Age did produce a pair of real female pirates whose deeds have become the stuff of legend.

Anne Bonny and Mary Read were two formidable women who sailed with the pirate Calico Jack Rackam. Bonny left a possessive husband to join Rackam as lover and fellow pirate. Mary Read was one of those remarkable eighteenth-century women who went to sea dressed as a man until her ship was taken by pirates in 1720. She revealed her secret to Bonny and the two women became the leading members of Rackam's crew. In fact, when a sloop specially fitted out by the Governor of Jamaica surprised their ship in 1720, Rackam and his men fled below. Only Read and Bonny fought back. Rackam and his men were hanged, but Read and Bonny were spared because they were both pregnant. Anne Bonny uttered a memorable epitaph

Above: Mary Read reveals herself as a disguised woman in duel. Right: Female pirates in the 18th century were often shown using turnoff pistols such as this elegant example.

about Rackam: "If he'd fought like a man, he need not have been hanged like a dog." Today, Bonny and Read continue to inspire many depictions of female pirates in film.

At the very end of the Golden Age of Piracy in Atlantic Canada, a resourceful and ruthless woman did appear on the decks of a gutted ship in Nova Scotia and successfully hoodwinked the colony's governor. Susannah Buckler was discovered alone aboard a looted ship named the *Baltimore* near Yarmouth, Nova Scotia, in May 1736.

Ann Bonny and Mary Read were spared as they were both pregnant. They continue to inspire many depictions of female pirates.

She said she was the wife of the captain and that he had been murdered, along with the rest of the crew, by Mi'kmaq. The Governor at Annapolis Royal, Lawrence Armstrong, believed her tale of woe and sent her off to Boston with letters of introduction and even spending money.

A few weeks later an embarrassing letter arrived from the real Susannah Buckler in Barbados seeking the fate of her husband. *Baltimore* turned out to be a convict ship and the woman found aboard was one Mrs. Mathews, an Irish convict who had helped take over the ship. The notorious Mrs. Mathews was a well-known thief and prostitute in Dublin. After her husband had been executed in 1735, she fought another woman who claimed to be his widow for possession of the body. A Dublin newspaper reported that they settled the dispute "in a fair combat which lasted about Half and Hour. At length the Conqueror was, by the Mob, declared the lawful Widow and carried off in great triumph."

However, by the time the furious Governor Armstrong learned that he'd been duped by this "vile imposter and piratical Murderer," she was long gone. Some of her fellow mutineers were eventually caught and tried in Boston, but Mrs. Mathews is believed to have returned to Ireland.

PIRATE FOLKLORE AND MYTH

They had a party, they soused him and buried him alive with the treasure.

Enos Hartlan, storyteller, Eastern Passage, 1928

In the spring of 1928, Helen Creighton sat spellbound at a kitchen table as an elderly man bewitched her with pirate songs and stories about pirates who would kill a man to guard their treasure with his cursed soul. That conversation inspired her career in Canadian folklore. Seeking pirate tales and pirate song led her to travel throughout Nova Scotia, collecting songs, stories and superstitions.

Everywhere she went she found storytellers with their own tales of pirate ghosts who guard treasure on Nova Scotian islands. The pattern described in her books *Bluenose Ghosts* and *Bluenose Magic* was remarkably consistent.

Pirates would trick one of their number to volunteer as a guard. He would be promptly killed and buried with the treasure, his ghost cursed to guard it until the pirates returned, or until brave treasure hunters could foil him. Treasure hunters need to follow magic rules. You can only dig at night because then you can spot the ghost guarding the treasure. Once you start digging, no one can talk because it gives extra powers to the pirate ghosts guarding the treasure. Magic tools such as shovels sprinkled with holy water or dowsing rods are recommended.

Told with endless creative variations, these yarns are a staple of the region's folklore. Each

island and each storyteller adds his own twist. Navy Island in Halifax's Bedford Basin is guarded not by one, but by a whole crew of pirates. Devil's Island, at the mouth of Halifax Harbour, used to have a pond where every seven years a treasure chest would rise to the surface. In Liverpool, it is a pack of giant cats that appear as guards. Near Apple River a headless ghost tries to persuade people to follow him and then turns into a ball of fire.

Other variations appear in New Brunswick locations. At St. Martins on the Bay of Fundy, a treasure myth holds that Isle Haute, far out in the bay, moves every seven years and should you be on the island at that time, a flaming headless ghost rises from the treasure site. Three luckless treasure hunters are said to have confronted this ghost in the nineteenth century, but it killed two of them and left the third insane. At Jacquet River on New Brunswick's North Shore, many people have seen in dreams the location of treasure on an island close to the shore. One group of treasure hunters had just unearthed a small cavern on the island when a ghostly vessel appeared, traversing the bay without oars or sails and even crossing sandbars.

Below: The replica privateer Pride of Baltimore II *approaches McNabs Island, home to a treasure legend like all of Nova Scotia's islands.*
Opposite: One of the many maps inspired by Robert Louis Stevenson, this Bay of Fundy treasure map by Julian Fish was a prize in a 1960 breakfast cereal box.

Capt. Edward Low his Treasure on Isle Haute

THE HEADLESS GHOST

ANCHORAGE

BAR

PIGEON POINT

TREASURE SITE

BOAR'S HEAD ROCK

SHEER CLIFFS

FLAT FIELD

OLD

TRIANGULAR POND

INDIAN

GRASSY SLOPE

FEASTING

SWAMP

STRAWBERRY PATCH

GROUND

PASTURE

OLD AXE

FOUND HERE

VICIOUS RIP TIDES

©Copyright
C. Julian Fish

BAY OF FUNDY

Low's Pirate Brigantine "Rebecca"

Low and his Three Companions Hanged at Martinique

Lithographed in Canada

At St. Martins on the Bay of Fundy, a treasure myth holds that Isle Haute, far out in the bay, moves every seven years and should you be on the island at that time, a flaming headless ghost rises from the treasure site. Three luckless treasure hunters are said to have confronted this ghost in the nineteenth century, but it killed two of them and left the third insane.

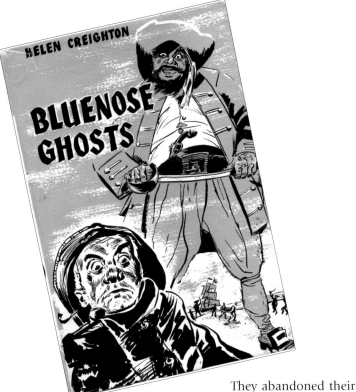

Pirate treasure legends persist in Newfoundland, especially in the old haunts of Peter Easton, where folklore holds that treasure is buried in every cove and cape he frequented. A number of ponds, too, are supposed to hide treasure. One in Red Bay was even drained by treasure hunters, while O'Darren's Island is said to be "bottomless" and requires magic to raise the treasure from the depths of its waters.

Newfoundland's most significant piece of Peter Easton folklore is the myth of the "Irish Princess" named Sheila O'Connor or Sheilagh NeGeira (Gaelic for Sheila the Beautiful). While travelling to a French convent, the Irish beauty was captured by Dutch pirates, who were in turn taken by Peter Easton in 1603. She fell in love with one of Easton's lieutenants, the dashing and handsome Gilbert Pike. The two were married by Easton himself. When Easton made his move from privateering to outright piracy in 1606, Pike chose not to take the pirate oath, but with Easton's blessing settled at Bristol's Hope. Sheila supposedly gave birth to the first English child born in Newfoundland and founded the large Pike family line in Newfoundland. Most historians, however, regard the story as an early twentieth-century invention. A gravestone in Carbonear, long claimed to mark Sheila Pike's grave, in fact marks the grave of a John and Juliana Pike from 1753.

Fake pirate stones are very common across Atlantic Canada. Helen Creighton catalogued their abundance in *Bluenose Ghosts*. One at Glen Margaret is marked "Kapt Kit." Another at Oak Island reveals "Kidd 200." In the Bay of Fundy, a stone on Isle Haute allegedly read "Captain Kidd—Gold and Jewels x fathoms east x fathoms down." Still another on White Island shows Kidd's name and hand pointing to the end of the island. Best of all is one near Marion Bridge, Cape Breton, shaped like a tombstone marked "Captain Kidd died without Mercy." These stones

They abandoned their digging. Even far up the Saint John River at Pokiok Falls, now submerged by the waters of Mactaquac Dam, treasure hunters were stopped in their digging by a corpselike ghost with a sword and cackling laughter.

Prince Edward Island has similar stories. Near North Cape, a treasure was supposed to have been buried under a gnarled old hawbush by the cliff's edge. However as soon as the treasure emerged, the guardian ghost would summon up the sound of galloping horses coming closer and closer until the treasure hunters cried out, causing the treasure to vanish. It is said that it will take a fearless deaf man to find the treasure.

Another "ghostly sounds" story comes from Maiden's Cave near Parrsboro, where a pirate named Deno supposedly sealed up a female captive in a cave with treasure. It is a story told with many variations. Some say that she stabbed him, others that she would not marry him, but all claim that her screams can still be heard near the rocky hollow and her shadowy figure sometimes crawls forth from cracks in the rocks.

still turn up, most recently in 1996 along the Kennebecasis River in New Brunswick with a stone marked "W. Kidd 1701." Creighton drolly raised the question of just why Captain Kidd would leave his name in so many places spelled so many different ways. The most well-known of these stones is the Captain Kidd pirate rock near Liscomb on Nova Scotia's Eastern Shore. It is featured as a clue in many Oak Island books. However, James S. Macdonald, a former president of the Royal Nova Scotia Historical Society admitted that he carved the stone in the late 1800s as a youthful prank.

Powerful pirate ghost stories obscure the fact that no one has convincingly found pirate treasure anywhere. Despite the myths, pirates almost never buried treasure. Their loot was quickly divided among the crew according to the pirate articles. Francis Drake briefly buried treasure while fleeing the Spanish in 1573, and there is one documented account of a merchant named Captain Stratton who bought bags of silver coins from pirates and briefly buried them at York River in Chesapeake Bay in 1720.

The main origin of the treasure legend was William Kidd. The treasure he captured in the Indian Ocean was, in typical pirate fashion, divided among his crew as they dispersed first at Madagascar, then in the West Indies and finally in New York. Most of Kidd's share was left — not buried — with a friend named John Gardiner on Long Island. Kidd tried to use his treasure as a bargaining chip after his arrest, but authorities zealously tracked down everyone he knew, seized the £14,000 of treasure and sent it off to England for his trial. It was eventually forfeited to the crown

Right: This map by Robert Louis Stevenson started it all. It inspired his novel and all subsequent tales of pirate treasure.
Opposite: The original cover to Helen Creighton's Bluenose Ghosts.

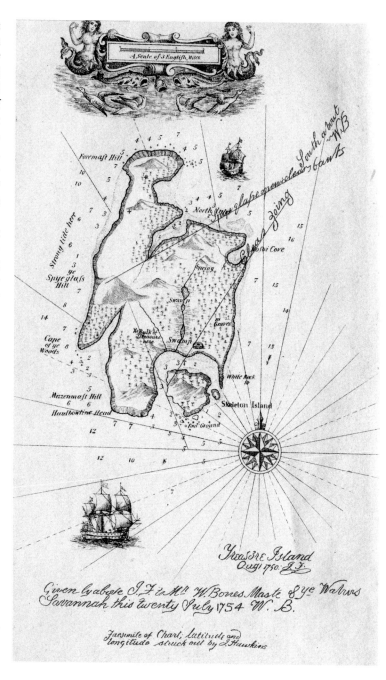

Above: Oak Island, the place in Nova Scotia that is associated with pirate legend more than any other. More than 50 books have been written on the subject. Opposite: An intricate summary by George T. Bates of Oak Island's fanciful theories and imaginary clues.

and was used to build the famous naval hospital at Greenwich in 1705. However, Kidd's desperate ploy convinced all manner of people that he must have buried more of it before his arrest.

The idea of treasure maps comes from Robert Louis Stevenson. He sketched an attractive romantic map full of secret clues for his great pirate novel *Treasure Island* in 1883. His map inspired so many souvenir copies and outright fake treasure maps that the Library of Congress actually published a whole book in 1965 entitled *A Descriptive List of Treasure Maps*, listing the hundreds of dubious treasure maps known to exist. One such map drew a writer and treasure hunter named Edward Snow to Isle Haute in the Bay of Fundy in 1952. Guided by the map — with murky origins but allegedly signed by the notorious pirate Ned Low — Snow reported that he had found several coins clutched in the hand of a skeleton buried on the island's beach. Believed by some to be a plant and by others to be coins from a shipwreck, the coins were photographed and featured in *Life* magazine. They were later stolen during a robbery at Snow's house.

Isle Haute may at least have produced something of value, which is more than can be said for the one place in Atlantic Canada more associated with pirate legend than any other: Oak Island. The hunt for treasure began in 1795 when three men noticed an odd depression on the island near Chester, Nova Scotia, and started

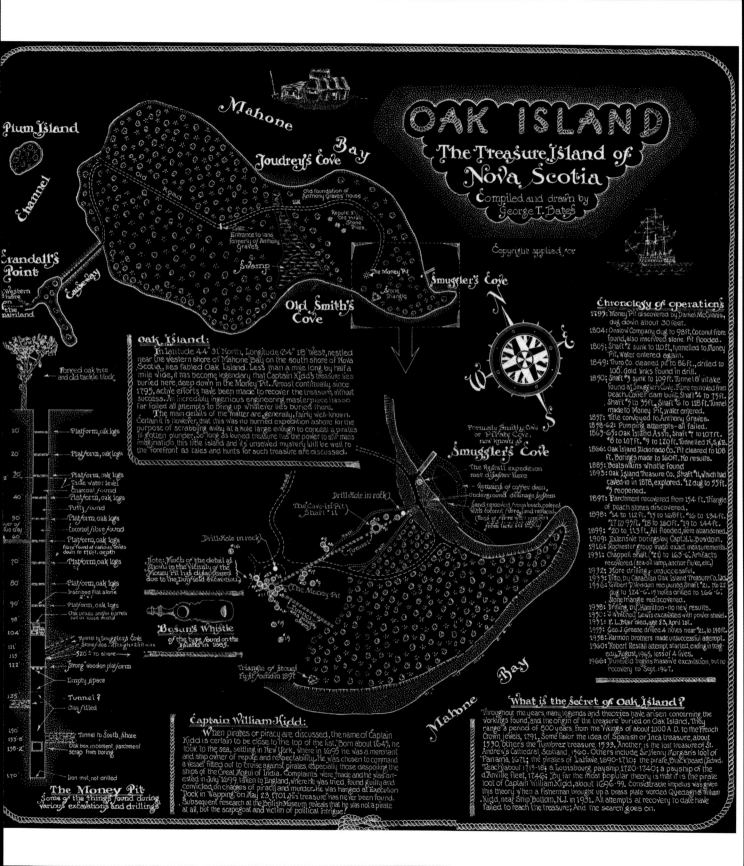

Above: One of many romantic and wealthy investors drawn to Oak Island was Franklin D. Roosevelt seen here on the island in 1910, third from the right.

🌀 *Opposite: Fragmentary clues from the Money Pit: reeds, coconut fiber and a shaft timber.*

digging. The hole was soon called the "Money Pit" and it has defeated the technology of every subsequent generation. The picks and shovels of the eighteenth century were soon replaced by the steam-driven pumps, pitheads and drill bits of the nineteenth century, followed by the bulldozers and open-pit mining of the twentieth century. None of these efforts yielded anything before being defeated by cave-ins and flooding. The Money Pit was destroyed and the island's 57 hectares are now riddled with pits and boreholes.

The persistent flooding and odd bits of wood and clay have convinced treasure hunters and writers that the island hides an elaborate engineering work of secret flood tunnels, multilayer platforms and hidden caverns. Each generation of treasure hunters has added its own embellishments to produce detailed cross-sections of the Money Pit. These are largely works of the imagination, based on the undocumented memories of a handful of nineteenth-century treasure hunters and tiny unverified fragments from drill bits. All the known treasure found on Oak Island has amounted to a few common coins and three links of gold chain or gold lace, none of which still exist today.

The treasure hunters on Oak Island point to a bizarre welter of clues and evidence. Some of the clues are mysterious, some are entertaining and most are easily explained as remnants from previous treasure hunters. One of the more bizarre and dubious of these clues is the "inscribed stone," covered with marks and scratches, supposedly found in the Money Pit in 1803. Somehow, although it was supposed to have existed into the twentieth century as a vital clue, no one ever photographed it or even traced the inscription before it disappeared. Only a crude sketch of the characters has ever surfaced, but that hasn't stopped amateur cryptologists from endlessly decoding it. "Forty Feet Below Two Million Pounds Are Buried" is the most popular translation.

One of the few hard-to-dismiss pieces of Oak Island evidence are coconut fibres, most of which appear to have been found on the beach at Smith's Cove. Some testing has confirmed that the fibres are indeed derived from coconut trees. Some treasure hunters feel they were used as a filter for the flood tunnels that protect the treasure. Skeptics suggest they are merely flotsam from coconut fibres, which were commonly used in the nineteenth century to pack cargo on ships.

Oak Island has produced no treasure, but it has created a rich and entertaining range of theories generated by both treasure hunters and authors. The first theories were all about pirates, shaped by the deep province-wide folklore of pirate treasure. William Kidd was the first suspect. Treasure hunters in the 1860s claimed that early settlers had met one of Kidd's crew in England who told them Kidd's treasure was buried on an island of oaks east of Boston. Later writers put forward Edward Teach (Blackbeard). For good measure, some threw in a possible alliance with the pirate William Avery. Henry Morgan also joined the list, with the suggestion that he hid the loot from his 1671 raid on Panama on the island.

There is no evidence that any of these pirates spent time in Nova Scotia. William Kidd never made it north of Boston when he returned from the Indian Ocean and Blackbeard never ventured north of Delaware. Ironically, none of the Oak Island theories have included pirates such as Bartholomew Roberts or Ned Low who actually did make several raids along the Nova Scotian coast. One land surveyor has suggested that the tunnels and shafts may have provided the drainage system for a pirate dry dock. Others have suggested that the island may have been a communal hiding spot for many pirates.

The pirate theories are rivalled by others that claim Oak Island engineering was so sophisticated, that it had to be a large secret government effort. It has been suggested that various French and British expeditions have buried everything from the loot taken during the British capture of Havana in 1762 to the crown jewels of Louis XVI, hidden from the French Revolution in 1789. More recently, theorists have suggested that the Massachusetts merchant and later governor, William Phips used Oak Island to hide treasure that he recovered from a Spanish shipwreck in 1687.

And then there are the exotic theories, such as the one suggested by an author in 1953 that the Elizabethan scientist and statesman Francis Bacon hid manuscripts at Oak Island that proved he wrote the plays of William Shakespeare. Several subsequent authors have suggested the island was used by Freemasons or exiled members of the Knights Templar for various secret purposes, including hiding the Holy Grail or clues or treasure related to the Grail.

Perhaps the least welcome theory about Oak Island is the suggestion that there is nothing there beyond common geology compounded by generations of treasure hunting. Much of the bedrock of the island is anhydrite, a type of limestone that often produces sinkholes. These natural pits can fill up with layers of logs, silt and clay deposited by storms. Such sinkholes have appeared on the island and on the nearby mainland in the twentieth century. Limestone can also create underground cavities and complicated underground water flows. Add the rusted and splintered remnants of two centuries of treasure hunting and you have an innocent explanation for most of what has been found on Oak Island.

While Oak Island has disappointed treasure hunters, it has rewarded authors and publishers, who have founded a publishing industry around the island. More than 50 books have been written about Oak Island, the first account in 1863 and the most recent in 2006.

Oak Island is also a resource for Nova Scotia's tourism industry. The island itself has seldom been open to the public and there is not all that much to see; it is really at its best when viewed from a distance, across the water — mysterious, overgrown and inaccessible. It is the story itself that is the lure. The Oak Island legend has been a staple of tourism guides to Nova Scotia since they were first published. Every guidebook, public and private, tells the familiar story using the legend of the island itself as an attraction to the region.

The lure of Oak Island treasure has also brought change to Nova Scotian law. In 1954 the Province created the Treasure Trove Act to regulate feuds between Oak Island treasure hunters. It set out a licensing system, whereby treasure hunters can keep 90 percent of whatever they find if they register their claims with the province of Nova Scotia. Other treasure hunters have convinced the courts to apply this law to Nova Scotian shipwrecks, which occasionally do contain some treasure, making Nova Scotia the only province in Canada to legalize treasure hunting.

Beyond the treasure theories, Oak Island has also generated a wealth of ghostly folklore, some of it with vivid and chilling imagery. A widely repeated belief is the prediction that the treasure will not be found until the deaths of those seeking treasure equal the mystic number of seven, and so far the island has claimed six lives. Locals have reported seeing strange lights and pillars of fire rising from the island. Others claim to have seen and photographed glowing orbs. A mysterious boat with eight oarsmen is said to appear from out of the mist. Some stories say that the sounds of pirate cutlasses and oaths can be heard.

A story collected by Helen Creighton from several sources tells of a ghost with a red coat who often appears offering cryptic clues of where to dig. Even more vivid are the island's ghostly guardians. Thunder is supposed to erupt when digging begins, growing louder and closer if it continues. A common report is the appearance of a large crow that circles overhead whenever a shovel is put into the ground on the island. An even more intimidating image is a huge black dog with fiery red eyes — the devil's watchdog — which is supposed to guard the treasure.

❸ *A 19th century Halifax "strong box" or money chest at the Maritime Museum of the Atlantic.*

PIRATES IN POPULAR CULTURE

Oh, better far to live and die,
Under the brave black flag I fly,
Than play sanctimonious part,
With a pirate head and pirate heart

The Pirate King, *The Pirates of Penzance*, Gilbert and Sullivan

The notoriety and romance of pirates has long fascinated the public, starting with eighteenth-century ballads, growing into Victorian adventure novels and followed by comic operas and plays. In the twentieth century, the romance and spectacle of pirates offered the Hollywood film industry one of its most popular and enduring genres, which has, in turn, influenced television, books, toys and theme parks.

The distorted and highly romanticized image of piracy that has evolved has little connection to its grim reality. However, these recently popularized portrayals sometimes echo the defiance and wild freedom that were part of piracy's eighteenth-century attraction.

Pirate songs have been popular for hundreds of years and reached huge audiences in the eighteenth and nineteenth centuries. Pirate ballads sometimes tell of unrepentant pirates, but they are most often "confessionals" where a pirate, about to be executed, warns others to avoid his cruel fate. Helen Creighton collected many such ballads sung by Ben Henneberry of Devil's Island. One of the oldest pirate songs is "Captain Kidd" written at the time of his execution in 1701. It contains the memorable lines,

"My name is Captain Kidd, God's laws I did forbid, And most wickedly I did, As I sailed, as I sailed". Revived many times, a pop version became a regional hit for the Newfoundland folk-rock group Great Big Sea in 2005.

The 1724 book *A General History of the Pirates* has influenced everything you have ever seen about famous pirates. Written during

Above: Poster for Gilbert and Sullivan's musical which began piracy's march from crime to harmless fun for children.
Opposite: Parrots are now synonymous with pirates thanks to Robert Louis Stevenson.

the Golden Age of Piracy, while many famous pirates were still alive and at large, it mixes history, journalism and rumour. The book condemns the vile deeds of pirates while also celebrating their notoriety. The identity of the author, Captain Charles Johnson, is a mystery. Some historians think the name was a pseudonym for Daniel Defoe, the famous author of *Robinson Crusoe*, but more recent scholarship has doubted this attribution. Some historians think Johnson may have been a pirate himself. In any case, he was remarkably well informed. His book has been reprinted countless times. Early editions included woodcuts that provided the first visual portraits of pirates.

Nova Scotian author William Gilkerson revisited Charles Johnson's history of piracy in his 2005 novel *Pirate's Passage*, which won the 2006 Governor General's Award for Children's Literature. It combined a serious history of piracy with the character of the mysterious Charles Johnson in the spirit of the pirate classic written by Robert Louis Stevenson, *Treasure Island*.

Authors in the nineteenth century transformed pirates from figures of notoriety and fear into figures of romance and myth. Lord Byron's epic poem *The Corsair* in 1814 and Walter Scott's novel *The Pirate* in 1821 both recast pirates as romantic rebel aristocrats. However, it was Robert Louis Stevenson who made the most powerful contribution to the romancing of the pirate. His 1883 novel *Treasure Island* gave the grim reality of piracy the completely fictional — but fun — features of secret maps, buried treasure, parrots and "pirate talk" with invented phrases like "shiver me timbers." In another pirate novel, Stevenson also popularized an image that made him beloved of Hollywood film directors — walking the plank. Pirates used all kinds of horrible ways to murder and torture people, but there are no accounts of real pirates in the 1700s making captives walk the plank. Described in his 1889 novel *The Master of*

Ballantrae, the notion of walking the plank exploded in popularity among theatre producers and film directors. It perfectly suited their requirements for high drama on a limited set that did not need elaborate special effects.

English theatre in fact had quickly embraced pirates, with a play in 1713 called *The Successful Pirate*, based on the pirate William Avery. Gilbert and Sullivan set out to parody many pirate dramas in 1879 when they created the light-hearted romance *The Pirates of Penzance*. J.M. Barrie's classic children's play *Peter Pan* in 1904 further developed the idea of pirates as harmless comic figures with the invention of Captain Hook and his bumbling crew.

If Robert Louis Stevenson's books established the conventions, the many historical novels of Rafael Sabatini, such as *The Black Pirate*, *Captain Blood* and *The Black Swan*, provided the swashbuckling plots. Their theatrical potential was first harnessed in spectacular fashion by Hollywood in the 1926 silent film *The Black Pirate* starring Douglas Fairbanks. From the beginning pirate films played mix and match with history.

Historical accuracy is usually limited to the use of roughly appropriate weapons from the Golden Age of Piracy, but everything else is a jumble: ships from one century, clothes from another.

These films almost never depicted real pirates nor real pirate events, but established their own fantasy conventions: dashing sword fights, aristocratic pirates and beautiful damsels in distress. Every generation finds its cinematic swashbuckler in this fantasy world: Errol Flynn as *Captain Blood* in 1935; Tyrone Power in the *Black Swan* in 1942 and Burt Lancaster as *The Crimson Pirate* in 1952.

Canadian film and television productions make occasional pirate references, but usually merely import the stereotypical Hollywood pirates into a Canadian setting. One exception is an overlooked 1989 gem by Salter Street Films entitled *Georges Island*, which integrated the region's unique folklore legends with Hollywood imagery in a lively way. The 2001 film *The Shipping News*, set in

Jim Simpson, a costumed tour boat employee inspired in equal parts by 17th century bucanneers and 20th century movies.

The most popular pirate title in film has been Stevenson's *Treasure Island*. Starting with a silent version in 1920, there have been more than 50 film and television adaptations including German, Soviet and Japanese versions, and, of course, *Muppet Treasure Island*. The conventions of pirate films — pirate talk, parrots and dimwitted sidekicks — have been repeated so often that more recent pirate films mine them for comedy.

The 2003 film *Pirates of the Caribbean* and its sequels ornamented piracy with the thickest romantic layers yet seen of magic, treasure and wild costumes. They are films inspired by a theme park ride, by other films, by novels and by real pirates — the latest links in a long evolutionary chain of pirate imagery. However, buried under all the special effects, romantic subplots and treasure, the fantasy film world of pirates does have at is heart an appeal that is the same as piracy's appeal to mariners in the 1700s.

Freedom and rebellion are the powerful lures of piracy. Romance sweetens and sanitizes the brutal side of pirate life, but the chance to escape and seek vengeance remains at the core.

Newfoundland, gave a vivid — if highly gothic — glimpse into the legends of the island's pirate wreckers.

PIRACY TODAY

The worst thing, for me, was that the bastards were smiling.

Canadian Gord Chaplin under pirate attack, 2005

Piracy became virtually unknown in Atlantic Canada in the twentieth century, limited to only the occasional minor theft of small vessels or the occasional burst of protest boat burnings, easily dealt with by the normal processes of criminal law enforcement.

Remarkably, during the explosion of smuggling in the Prohibition era of the 1920s, little piracy existed. In contrast to the vicious gangster wars fought over the retail of illegal alcohol in American cities, very few hijackings and almost no violence occurred at sea amidst the fleet of hundreds of vessels smuggling alcohol to the coasts of America.

The last outburst of piracy in the region was a bizarre series of fishing boat thefts in the late 1960s. It began the day before Christmas in 1965 when the 48-foot wooden fishing boat *Ernest and Ronald* disappeared from the wharf at Lockport on Nova Scotia's South Shore. The boat was found a day later, 100 miles offshore with one man aboard. He had stolen the boat as a lark.

Two years later, another Lockport fisherman stole an even larger fishing dragger. Bruce Moore worked aboard the dragger *Cape Spry*, but was unhappy about wages and working conditions.

Top: Sailors from HMCS Winnipeg *search a suspected pirate skiff, Gulf of Aden, 2009.*

☯ *Bottom: The trawler* Hansen, *stolen in 1961 by one of the lasts acts of piracy in Canada.*

On St. Patrick's Day, after a night of drinking, he stole *Cape Spry* and smashed his way out of a crowded wharf. Piloting the 92-foot vessel — normally operated by 12 men — by himself through a gale of snow, freezing spray and high

winds, he eluded a series of Canadian and American Coast Guard vessels and military aircraft for three days. The Canadian Coast Guard vessel *Thomas Carleton* finally captured the runaway fishing boat on March 20.

The bold voyage made the affable 23-year-old Moore into a bit of a folk hero. Charges of piracy were reduced to theft and he drew a two-year jail sentence. However, the copycat pirates were not over yet. Just two days later, William Atwood and William Jacklyn stole the 84-foot dragger *Hansen* from the wharf at Shelburne and made it 40 miles offshore before an RCMP patrol boat caught them, 12 hours later. For the region's last major act of piracy, they too went to jail for two years.

However, vessels and mariners that venture from Nova Scotia to the ocean highways of the world still face the very real threat of piracy in many places. Piracy is not only still with us: it actually blossomed in the late twentieth century. Some blame its resurgence on the epidemic of armed attacks on the helpless refugee "boat people" who fled Vietnam in the late 1970s. By the 1980s, a few dozen pirate attacks took place every year. The end of the Cold War in 1991 was followed by a huge increase in global trade, almost all of it shipped by water, and this has fed piracy with an unprecedented supply of victims.

According to the International Chamber of Commerce, worldwide pirate attacks since 1995 have averaged about 200 per year, peaking in some years such as 2004, when 329 pirate attacks killed 30 mariners. The surprising prevalence of piracy today stems from one of the realities of global trade. So many of the cheap consumer and luxury goods that we take for granted in the West are made in the East and travel through waters where terrible poverty exists ashore. It should be no surprise that a small fraction of this trade falls prey to piracy.

Most attacks are quick raids by heavily armed

The cruise ship Seabourn Spirit *in Halifax a few months before being attacked by pirates.*

men in fast boats who take money and luxury goods in "maritime mugging" style raids. However, some crews are held for ransom, and in other chilling attacks entire crews disappear. Their ships reappear, registered under new names with the collusion of corrupt officials. Yachts, fishing boats and small cargo ships are the usual victims, but pirates sometimes target large container ships and even cruise ships.

A regular caller to the ports of St. John, Halifax, Sydney and St. John's is the *Seabourn Spirit*, a mid-sized cruise ship that caters to the luxury market of regional cruises. After a visit that took the 300 passengers to the game parks of Kenya, it was attacked by pirates off the coast of Somalia on November 5, 2004. Speedboats launched from a rusty trawler peppered the ship with machine-gun fire and rocket-propelled grenades. The captain was able to use speed and a piercing acoustic device to escape from the pirates without injury. Not so lucky are the cargo freighters that are regularly robbed or held for ransom by Somali pirates almost every month. Sailors in the Canadian Navy, who grew up with

pirates in film and television, now routinely prepare to fight them when their duties take them to African and Middle Eastern waters.

All the oceans of the world see occasional attacks, but the most dangerous areas have become the waters around Indonesia and the Philippines, followed by the east and west coast of Africa and parts of South America. The Straits of Malacca in Indonesia see some of the heaviest levels of commercial shipping in the world and suffered an epidemic of pirate attacks in the 1990s. The raids have declined only recently, partially due to the 2004 Boxing Day Tsunami, which wiped out many pirate communities in the Straits. However, much as piracy in the Golden Age would spread from one continent to another, piracy soon increased in Nigeria and most spectacularly off the coast of Somalia.

In these places, the reasons for piracy are the same as they were in 1700s. Combine rich trade routes with poverty, political strife, corrupt governments and weak navies, and you can expect pirates.

FURTHER READING

Piracy has an enormous body of literature. The following sources are an introduction to the essentials, with a focus on the pirates of Atlantic Canada.

Donald Chard, *"The Last Voyage of the Baltimore,"* Nova Scotia Historical Review (1987).
A carefully researched account of the stranger-than-fiction story of Mrs. Mathews.

Dan Conlin, *"The Golden Age of Piracy in Nova Scotia: Three Case Studies,"* Journal of the Royal Nova Scotia Historical Society, Vol. 12, 2009.
A more formal scholarly presentation of the pirate research behind this book.

David Cordingly, *Under the Black Flag: The Romance and the Reality of Life Among the Pirates* (Harcourt Brace & Company, 1995).
A recent account with an especially valuable look at pirate popular culture.

Helen Creighton, *Bluenose Ghosts* (Ryerson Press, 1957; Nimbus Publishing, 1994).
Contains a fascinating chapter on pirate folklore.

George Francis Dow and John Henry Edmonds, *The Pirates of the New England Coast 1630-1730* (Marine Research Society, 1923; reprinted by Dover Publications, 1996).
Well-researched accounts of the Golden Age pirates, not just in New England but also Nova Scotia and Newfoundland.

William Gilkerson, *Pirate's Passage* (Trumpeter Books, 2006).
A history of pirates told within a novel inspired by the mysterious Charles Johnson.

Philip Gosse, *The Pirates' Who's Who* (Burt Franklin Press, 1924).
A delightful concept and indispensable reference.

Olaf Janzen, *"The Problem of Piracy in the Newfoundland Fishery,"* 7th Conference for the History of the Northern Seas (1994).
The only scholarly study of Newfoundland piracy.

Charles Johnson, *A General History of the Pirates* (Rivington, 1724).
The classic period-source for the Golden Age of Pirates. Many later editions have been published, some attributed to Daniel Defoe.

Archibald MacMechan, *Sagas of the Sea.* (J. M. Dent & Sons, 1923).
Classic accounts of Edward Jordan and the *Saladin* pirates.

Marcus Rediker, *Villains of All Nations: Atlantic Pirates in the Golden Age* (Beacon Press, 2004).
A social and political analysis of the beliefs and way of life of pirates.

Robert C. Ritchie, *Captain Kidd and the War Against the Pirates* (Harvard University Press, 1986).
A carefully researched biography of Kidd, placing him in the evolution of piracy.

Robert Louis Stevenson, *Treasure Island* (Cassell & Company, 1883).
The book that set all the pirate conventions in book and film. It has been reprinted many times.

INDEX

PHOTO CREDITS

Canadian Navy: 92t; Dan Conlin: 19; Danielle Langlois: 15b; Estate of George T. Bates: 83; From the Collection of the Maritime Museum of the Atlantic, Halifax: front cover photo & 59b; Gerry Lunn, gibbet replica John Tate; 5; M2008.17.1w model made by Frank Wilson, 42; M60.50, 57b; exhibit photo by Gerry Lunn, 58t; 59l; M2006.16.1, 60; 64r; M60.46, 65; MP3.50.8, 66tr; MP3.50.11, 66cr; MP3.50.6, 66br; M2004.50.91a-e, 85; M92.55.1, 86; MP15.4.1, 92b; Government of Nova Scotia: 82t; Halifax Army Museum: 15t, 25, 51t, 52, 71l, 71r, 74, 75b; Howard Pyle: 10, 17, 20, 27b, 68-69, 73r; iStock: 6, 7, 9, 11, 15b, 21, 22l, 23, 26t, 26b, 28, 30, 31, 33, 36t, 37, 38, 41, 44, 45b, 46, 47, 49, 50, 51, 53, 54, 55, 59t, 62l, 64l, 67, 68l, 70, 72c, 77, 78t, 78b, 87, 88b, 89, 90, 91; Ken MacLean: 45t, 79; Kent State University Special Collections and Archives: 62; Mac McKay Shipfax: 93; Mary Evans Picture Library: 32, 75t, 88t; Musée des Beaux-Arts, Rouen: 39; National Maritime Museum (London): 12t; Nova Scotia Archives and Records Management: NSARM Map Collection–*Atlantic Neptune* S29 N30, 34-35; NSARM Art Collection–1979-147.612, 57t; NSARM Photo Collection–Ships–Herbert Fuller, 66l; Nova Scotia Museum, Archaeology Collection, Halifax: back cover assorted shipwreck coins, 12b, 14l, 22r, 27t; Nova Scotia Museum, History Collection: 14r, 58b, 61, 72b; Robert Louis Stevenson: 81; US National Franklin D. Roosevelt Library: 84; William Gilkerson: 36b, 73l.